Propaganda

Anthony Rhodes

EDITED BY
Victor Margolin

PRODUCED
AND ART DIRECTED BY
Harris Lewine

Volume 2

Chelsea House Publishers
New York   London

Rhodes, Anthony Richard Ewart.
Propaganda: the art of persuasion in WW II.

Filmography: p.
1. World War, 1939–1945—Propaganda.
2. Propaganda—History. I. Title.
D810.P6R48   940.54'88   75-17545

ISBN 0-87754-463-8 (vol. 2)
0-87754-461-1 (set)

Design: Seymour Chwast

Chelsea House Publishers
Harold Steinberg, Chairman & Publisher
Susan Lusk, Vice President
A Division of Chelsea House Educational Communications, Inc.
133 Christopher Street, New York 10014

Contents

Volume 2

CHAPTER FIVE

RULE AND RESISTANCE IN 'THE NEW ORDER' 1936-1945

"France has lost a battle;
she has not lost the War."
CHARLES DE GAULLE
*Broadcast from London to Occupied France,
June 18, 1940.*

When in 1936 Hitler repudiated the treaties of Versailles and Locarno and marched his troops into the Rhineland, he took a calculated risk. He knew that if the French marched too, he was lost. But he did not think the French would attack him; and he was right. The French and their British allies wanted peace at any price. This was confirmed when the Spanish Civil War began three months later. The Western powers postulated the farce of nonintervention, which Hitler and Mussolini, now openly contemptuous of them, brazenly flouted. They found the Civil War a most convenient testing ground for their new weapons, which Goebbels justified by making great play of the atrocities allegedly committed by the Reds in Spain—the torture of nuns and hostages, the killing of children, the destruction of churches, convents, and religious shrines. He warned the world that Spain was being used by the Bolsheviks as a base for an attack on Western Europe. The liberals in England and France, as usual, did not see the danger. Goebbels presented the Fascist powers as upholding European civilization in Spain against the forces of "Jewish Bolshevism"; Germany had eradicated this cancer at home in 1933, and would now be proud to lead a crusade to help other countries do so. In every way Spain proved to be an excellent dress rehearsal for the much bigger "crusade" Germany was to lead in 1941 against the cradle of Bolshevism.

In the three years 1936–1939, Nazi foreign propaganda was to foster with every means in its power the defeatism which was revealed in France at the time of the Popular Front, so that France would at the moment of Hitler's choosing fall into German hands without a struggle. Hitler wanted to avoid wasting force on the Western powers if he could neutralize them by other means. He would reserve his military strength for the inevitable struggle in the East with the tough Soviet army. As he said to Rauschnigg, "Why should I bother to use military means, if I can do it better and more cheaply in other ways? . . . if I can break down the enemy psychologically before the armies begin to function at all? . . . By provocation of unrest in French public opinion, France can easily be brought to the point where she will be able to use her army too late, or not at all." In due course, all this came to pass. Hitler overcame France in six weeks, with military losses smaller than those Germany had sustained in a single battle of World War I. In this success, the machinations of Goebbels played a cardinal role.

One of his propagandists was Otto Abetz, a personable German who professed a great affection for France. In the years immediately before 1938 he lived in Paris, posing as an advocate of Franco-German understanding. Moving easily in Parisian society, he found a ready audience for his proposal that differences between the two countries should be settled amicably. Germany, he said, had absolutely no quarrel with France, nor designs on Alsace-Lorraine; all that was over, the 1914 war forgotten. Playing on anti-Semitism and anticommunism, he convinced many influential and patriotic Frenchmen that German and French interests could be identified.

(Top) "England, this is your work." A 1938 German poster in Poland shortly after the occupation. (Middle) "Monster, you made us suffer." This German poster for Belgium blamed the war on Churchill. (Bottom) The "falling leaf" which the Germans dropped on Parisians during the phony war. "The leaves fall because of God but you will fall because of the English."

In the early months of the war, German propagandists discovered how to create anti-Semitic propaganda by reversing the title of the London newspaper, The Times. (Top) An anti-British postcard. (Bottom) The "puzzle" leaflet was a later version of the same idea. The fragments were dropped on French soldiers in the Maginot Line.

War -„Times"

The next propaganda move was to divide France from her ally, Great Britain. Here Abetz and his French friends had the support of eminent French writers like Marcel Déat, whose theme was, "Why should we die for Danzig—because Britain has guaranteed Poland?" The French government was "the tool of British diplomacy," and the British would always "fight to the last Frenchman." All this became much more virulent during the Phony War in 1939–40. From the radio studios in Stuttgart, Goebbels' man Ferdonnet poured out a flood of propaganda asking why the British had only a few thousand troops in France, while France had mobilized her whole manpower in millions? He told the French that the British troops were much better paid than the French soldiers, which gave them the advantage for the favors of French women. In the weeks before the attack of May 1940, millions of German leaflets dropped on France showed the tired and dirty French poilu at the front, while the British soldier lay in the arms of French prostitutes well behind the lines. The most famous of these leaflets was "The Falling Leaf," actually shaped like a leaf, which littered the streets of northern French cities. Its legend above the death's head of a French poilu was "The leaves fall because God wills it—but we shall fall because the English will it. Next spring no one will remember either the leaves fallen this year, nor the French soldier fallen this year. Life will pass over our tombs . . ."

Against all this during the Phony War, the Western Allies were badly prepared. The British Ministry of Information was not yet in working operation; and no Ministry of Information existed in France until the May–June crisis of 1940. The French case was hardly presented at all, and when it was, its advocates seemed always on the defensive, trying to refute some piece of German propaganda, using such phrases as, "It's not true that . . ." or "It is inexact that . . . ," which only drew more attention to the German allegations. Until the 1940 crisis, the French director of information was the playwright Jean Giraudoux, of whom de Rochemont, the Paris correspondent of *Life*, wrote, "His feeling about Germany is comparable to that of a brother whose sister has gone on the streets and developed homicidal tendencies. He is full of pity, terror, to some extent shame—but mostly of sorrow."

In March 1940 Giraudoux's *Ondine* was the most popular play in Paris. It told of an immortal maiden beneath the sea, wooed by a mortal prince to the chagrin of her father and other submarine folk. The legend was really another verison of the *Rheingold* story. *Ondine* seemed to attract the Parisians in the same rather surprising way that Wagner did. Was such a man as Giraudoux a worthy opponent of Goebbels?

Goebbels' propaganda to France leading up to May 10, 1940, had been carefully planned. As Hitler had said earlier to Rauschnigg, "The place of artillery preparation will be taken by propaganda, before the armies arrive . . . mental confusion, indecision, panic, these are the first weapons. When the enemy is thoroughly demoralized from within, when social unrest is rife, that is the right moment. A single blow will then suffice." It did.

The problem for the Nazis after June 1940 was to govern the huge territories they had annexed so rapidly—France, the Low Countries, Denmark and Norway, as well as half of Poland—while preparing the final blow against Britain. Here propaganda, they knew, would be less effective in undermining the will to resist. Against an island people they would have to employ more material means; this was why they now tried to enlist France as an ally in the projected invasion.

Although the German press and radio had often discussed plans for the reorganization of Europe after the final victory, no serious attempt had been made to describe how the "New Order" was to operate—until July 1940, when the Nazi minister of economics, Walter Funk, went into the matter in some detail. From his speech it was immediately clear that the Nazis were primarily interested in the commercial exploitation of the occupied territories, and that all the grand talk about the New Order was mystification. The Germans wanted a continent at peace, self-sufficient economically and completely self-contained politically, in which the Greater German Reich would exercise hegemony.

The immediate problem was to present this *Grossdeutsche Reich* as offering France a prominent role in a noble enterprise on behalf of all Europe. Before the war and during the Phony War, the Goebbels propagandists had done all they could to divide the French among themselves, to put class against class. But after the fall of France and during the Occupation, they exhorted the French to pull together and forget their mutual antagonisms and class hatreds, in short to emulate Germany and the German virtues of hard work and sobriety; to work for collaboration, not revenge. Had not Germany, they asked, been exceptionally magnanimous to France in defeat, leaving her in possession of her navy and her colonies? While the British had, as usual, abandoned France in her hour of need. At Dunkirk, the British forces had been evacuated first, and the French were left to sit on the beaches waiting for death or captivity. A contemporary German cartoon shown in France had twin pictures, one of which shows a British Tommy and a French poilu standing together at the edge of a blood-filled swimming pool, poised to dive in. The British soldier is counting, "Ready? One . . . two . . . " The second picture shows the poilu, having dived in, floundering about and gulping, while the British Tommy is still standing on the edge, grinning and shouting, "Three!"

Posters on the walls of Paris and the provincial cities recalled the treatment meted out to France throughout the centuries by the hereditary enemy, "perfidious Albion." One of them, entitled *"L'appetit du dogue Britanique"* ("The appetite of the British bulldog"), showed a voracious looking bulldog, his jaws clamped on the world's Western hemisphere, which was marked with the names of the various territories taken from the French since early times. "England!" ran the caption, "YESTERDAY —in the 14th century she devastated Gascony . . . she burned Joan of Arc at Rouen . . . she stole French possessions in Canada, India, the West Indies, Malta. . . . she left Napoleon to rot on Saint Helena. . . . she humiliated France at Fashoda and

(Top left) During the phony war, cartoonists warned the French public against Hitler's tyranny. (Top, right) "Silence, the enemy is listening," a 1938 poster by Paul Colin. (Middle) A poster by Jean Carlu promoting Anglo-French solidarity, 1939. German propaganda at that time tried to drive a wedge between the two countries. (Bottom) French propaganda before the German invasion could still mock Hitler.

(Top, left) The Germans pasted this poster on Belgian walls. It condemned the British and Canadian troops for the attack on Dieppe in August 1942. (Top, right) "Don't forget Oran," a German poster seen in Paris after the British sank the French fleet at Oran. (Bottom) Anti-Semitic films like The Eternal Jew *were shown in Holland and other occupied countries.*

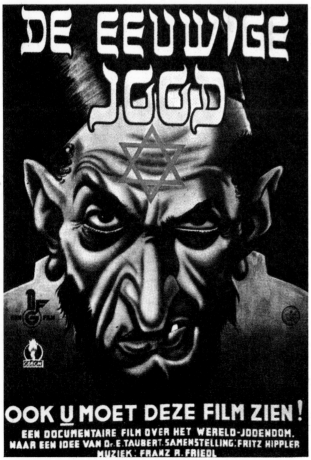

expelled her from Egypt . . . TODAY—she causes French blood to flow at Mers-el-Kebir, at Dakar, at Gabon, in Syria, Madagascar . . . TOMORROW—what new robbery and French bloodletting is she planning . . . ?"

Here, the British destruction of the French fleet at Mers-el-Kebir in July 1940 was an unexpected windfall for Goebbels. Posters were immediately placarded all over France showing a despairing French sailor drowning in the harbor of Oran, still clutching the tricolor. Another showed Churchill as an octopus, his tentacles stretching out to glean any possible prey.

This Nazi propaganda had some effect in Vichy, where the ministers around Pétain tended to be Anglophobe, and on that considerable portion of the French public for whom Pétain was regarded with almost religious veneration as the savior of France. In the later months of 1940, it was therefore possible to obtain some results from the "perfidious Albion" propaganda. But to present the Germans, if not the Nazis, as friends and confederates of the French proved somewhat harder. One of the most ubiquitous posters of this time in occupied France showed a tall, clean-cut, chivalrous looking Wehrmacht soldier comforting a young French widow with her children, taking them fondly in his strong arms; below was the caption, "Abandoned French populations! Have confidence in the German soldier!" Another poster celebrated the advantages of volunteering for work in Germany. It showed a poor French woman saying to her ragged children as she opened a letter from her husband in Germany, "Look! Now at last we have some money from him!" An attempt was even made to present Hitler as a simple soul, humble in his triumphs, tearful over his wounded soldiers, also a child lover. But this never really caught on.

The cinema was of course used freely by Goebbels as a propaganda medium. He founded a special French production company, the Continental, to make films for French consumption, on which he spent vast sums of money. His department supervised all branches of the French film industry—studios, printing works, production, distribution, publicity, even movie houses. This last led to the acquisition of many cinemas belonging to Jews; by 1944 one-third of the French film industry was in German hands. All film scripts had to pass two censorship bodies, the German and the Vichy. A typical example was *Les inconnus dans la maison (The Unknowns in the House)*, a film adaptation of a prewar Simenon novel, about a young Jewish maiden who perverts a good provincial bourgeoise and leads her from the straight and narrow path. But this sort of propaganda was too obvious for the French, as was *Jew Süss* and *Ohm Kruger,* and they tended to boycott such programs.

Pétain and his regime endeavored to convey to the French people the notion that France had sinned in the lotus years of the 1920s and '30s, that the defeat of 1940 was a condign, even divine, retribution. To account for French depravity in these years, Vichy adduced a host of curious reasons—contraception and the low birth rate, gambling, the immoral writing of Marcel Proust and André Gide, Pernod, permanent waves, bathing suits

... In the atmosphere of almost permanent self-castigation after June 1940, the aged marshal's cry of *"Travail! Famille! Patrie!"* ("Work, Family, Fatherland")—which replaced the traditional *"Liberté! Egalité! Fraternité!"*—seemed to sound a new and healthier note. To show how the country had changed for the better, a film was made to contrast the new "clean" life under Vichy with that in the decadent Anglo-Saxon countries. The French cineasts obtained a number of American newsreels and documentaries about life in New York; they selected certain episodes about speakeasies, nightclubs, call girls and the like, strung them together and released the film in France under the sardonic title *La Libre Amérique* (*America the Free*). The trouble was, however, that the French public, far from being shocked, was delighted with *La Libre Amérique*; they flocked to see it not for edification, but for vicarious pleasure.

Pétain's savior image was encouraged by the German propaganda machine. The poet Valéry-Larbaud compared Pétain resurrecting France with Christ resurrecting Lazarus; and a religious postcard showed two adjacent medallions, one bearing the effigy of Christ, the other of Pétain. When Paul Claudel's play *L'Annonce faite à Marie* (*The Annunciation to Mary*) was performed in Vichy, the dramatist wrote a laudatory ode to the marshal.

When after a year of Nazi-Pétain collaboration the war in Russia began, the Nazis thought they had a trump card in the large anti-Bolshevik element in occupied countries. Their propaganda now took the dual form of "Utopia round the corner," in a Europe under German "protection," and "Europe as a slave camp" if the Soviets won. When representatives of the Axis powers, their satellites, and sympathizers from Vichy France and other occupied countries gathered in Berlin in November 1941, it was to celebrate the "New Order in Europe" as a European crusade against Bolshevism. The Légion Volontaire Française was formed for those Frenchmen who believed in it, and were prepared to fight alongside the Germans in Russia. In commemoration of the occasion, the German radio stations broadcast a new "Song of Europe," and the Nazis issued a special stamp inscribed "European United Front against Bolshevism," against a background of a Europe decorated with a sword and a swastika. It was at this time in 1942 that Goebbels coined the term "Iron Curtain" (popularly and erroneously ascribed to Winston Churchill in his Fulton speech after the war). Goebbels told the occupied countries of Western Europe that if Germany did not destroy the Soviet Union, an "Iron Curtain" would descend over all Europe, separating its ancient and glorious civilization from the rest of the world. When in 1941 England espoused the cause of Soviet Russia, Goebbels deplored the ignorance of the British who had not learned the lesson of Kerenski.

For about six months all this crusade propaganda had some effect in Western Europe, but it never took real root and, after the first German reverses in the snows of the East, it began to lose its attraction. The Scandinavian countries, near neighbors

(Top, left) A poster announcing a rally of the Nasjonal Samling, the Norwegian Nazi movement led by Vidkun Quisling. (Top, right) A Nasjonal Samling recruiting poster, "Fight with Heroes." (Middle) An anti-German leaflet from Belgium. (Bottom) Poster columns such as this one in Holland were plastered with German propaganda during the occupation.

OSLO 1·2. NOV.

KJEMP MED HIRDEN

Belgian Worker, Come and work in Germany! Highest Wages and Safety, Splendid Food, Grand Amusements!

J. COCKERILL & CO

NO

(Top) During the Nazi occupation of Holland, a strong resistance movement and underground press affirmed the Dutch loyalty to Queen Wilhelmina. Underground papers ranged from simple stenciled sheets to handsomely printed journals. This cartoon was published in a clandestine magazine, De Groene Amsterdammer. (Bottom) A symbol of occupied Holland drawn by an Australian cartoonist.

of the Soviet Union, might still lend an ear to it; but the French people were too cynical to be taken in by it.

After the Wehrmacht's initial "correctness" in France, which had a limited success, the SS and the Gestapo spoiled it all with their Draconian measures. They began the fatal policy of executing hostages in retribution for German soldiers killed by the French Résistance. Their crude anti-Semitism had no appeal to a people which had once been divided by the Dreyfus affair. Particularly appalling was the Vélodrome d'Hiver episode, when Laval rounded up tens of thousands of French Jews for dispatch to the extermination camps in the East.

In other parts of Europe overrun by the Nazis, strenuous attempts were made, as in France, to woo the people to the cause of the New Order. In both Norway and Belgium, the Germans established pro-Nazi movements under Quisling and Degrelle respectively, which had some initial success. In Holland, where the Dutch Nazi party was headed by Anton Mussert, the Germans took over the Hilversum radio, using as a broadcaster Max Blokzijl, a conservative journalist who eloquently preached the Nazi gospel. Although known as "Lying Max" by the patriots, his programs nevertheless had a wide following. Another popular Nazi radio program in Holland for a while was a political cabaret which ridiculed the Allies and their Dutch supporters. In the first year of the occupation these efforts made some headway, and a number of volunteers from the occupied countries enlisted in the Waffen SS for service in Russia.

Broadly, one may say that the German propaganda to the occupied countries failed. It had worked well enough for years before the war, most effectively in preparing the military offensives in the West, acting as "softening-up" artillery on the enemy—that is to say acting negatively. But when the Nazis were confronted with the more prosaic business of administering the conquered territories, of winning the hearts and minds of the populations, they had nothing positive to offer. The fault lay not in Goebbels' propaganda, but in the very nature of National Socialism itself. After the military victories had been won, it was found to be barren. There was nothing to propagate, except stale racial theories which had no place in the modern world, where communications had brought people closer together than ever before. The New Order was a vision not of a brave new world, but of something resurrected from the mists and fogs of the Niebelungen.

"Propaganda," according to Maurio Megret, "takes as its objective the mind of the enemy, and makes use of the intellect *to compensate for the inadequacy of material resources.* It is therefore the weapon par excellence of the weak." This might well apply to the occupied countries in the early days. Organized resistance was not so much weak as nonexistent. Everything had happened too quickly. Isolated, unknown to one another, the potential resisters' only weapon was psychological. For over a year, France had no unified or disciplined resistance group. The first acts of resistance were therefore individual, by men and women acting on their own initiative. Their only value in 1940 and 1941 was that these small acts, if repeated, irritated the Germans—irritated rather than harrassed them—making them feel uncomfortable, aware that they were living in a hostile environment. When the first men of the Résistance daubed the letters RAF, or the V sign, or the Cross of Lorraine on the walls and pavements of Paris, they were obeying one of the basic rules of psychological warfare—to inform the enemy that, although he may have the upper hand militarily, he is surrounded by hostile, elusive, and immeasurable forces. Springing up ubiquitously and irregularly, these symbols were also an affirmation to other resistance groups that they were not alone.

In the early days after the western blitzkrieg, these spontaneous acts were puny and unplanned. At Bar-le-Duc, the secretary general of the department flew the French flag at half-mast and refused to take it down. A mayor in Seine-et-Oise stopped the town-hall clock to show that he did not recognize "the new time." In Chartres, the prefect instructed all mayors not to hang German notices on the walls of their offices. In Alsace, where German was understood and where German official notices for the civil population were appearing everywhere, they were defaced. The last six letters of the instruction *Achtung! Verdunkelung!* (Attention! Blackout!) were obliterated, so that the notice read, *Achtung! Verdun!* The word *offen* (open) on the compartment windows of trains was amplified into *Hoffen* (hope). *Raucher* (smoking compartment) on the trains became *Rache* (revenge). One journalist always made the same typing error in republishing material fed to him by the Gestapo; he continually referred to Hitler's masterwork as *Mein Krampf* (my cramp). Assemblies being forbidden in occupied France on the traditional public holidays (July 14, May 1, etc.), people foregathered spontaneously at the last moment, as if by chance, before the municipal war memorials. In all offices and factories, work would suddenly cease for a minute.

It was the same in the other occupied countries. In Holland, the Nazis had forbidden all official and semiofficial references to the exiled royal family, the House of Orange. Opposition to this was expressed in the pins and pendants made from the proscribed coinage bearing Queen Wilhelmina's head. The Dutch also often displayed or carried orange flowers. A favorite piece of wall propaganda used by the Dutch resistance was the number six and a quarter with a slash through it (6¼). This was a play on the Dutch *seis en kwart* (six and a quarter) and Seyss-Inquart, the chief Nazi occupation official in the Netherlands.

In Poland, a senior SS officer in the Government General named Moder was always referred to by the Poles as *Mörder* (murderer). On the walls of Warsaw the Nazi slogan *Deutschland siegt an allen Fronten* (Germany is victorious on all fronts) became *Deutschland liegt an allen Fronten* (Germany is prostrate on all fronts). In Brussels the annual parade at the tomb of the unknown soldier of the 1914 war was banned, so that day the Belgians marched past the Column of Congress, the monument to national independence. When this too was forbidden, students

(Top) A Belgian resistance sticker opposing Leon Degrelle's pro-Nazi Rexist movement. The demands of indigenous Nazi groups were ignored by the Germans, who relied on physical force rather than ideology to maintain the New Order. (Bottom) Posters such as this one for a German film were daubed with anti-Nazi drawings and slogans by resistance propagandists.

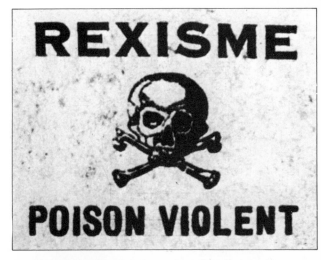

Variations on the Allied use of the "V for Victory" theme. (Top) A rebus with Churchill's cigar, Roosevelt's cigarette, and Stalin's pipe. (Second row, left) Churchill made the V sign famous. (Third row, left) A British cartoon reinforcing the V for Victory idea. (Opposite page) Paul Henried as the Czech underground leader, Victor Laslo, in Michael Curtiz's Casablanca *(1942).*

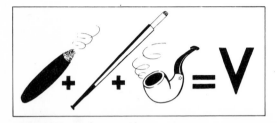

boarded trams which passed the column, made them slow down while they passed and threw out flowers at the foot of the column.

The most effective form of passive resistance was the V sign. Two Belgians working for the BBC Foreign Service knew that their countrymen at home, listening night after night to the British bombers overhead on their way to the Ruhr, often scrawled on factory walls the cheering letters RAF. But to write these clearly could take time, during which they might be arrested. The Belgians in London therefore invented for their own bilingual people (Walloon and Flemish) a simpler sign, the letter V, which stood for *victoire* for the French speaking Walloons, and *vrijheid* for the Flemish. It could be daubed on walls and pavements in a second. They suggested it to the deputy editor of the BBC, "Colonel Britton," who agreed that it should be tried out in Belgium. It was so successful that it was recommended to other occupied countries. Soon the V sign was appearing all over occupied Europe—even in countries where the word for victory does not begin with a V. Thus, in Czechoslovakia, V recalled the words of the great Czech patriot Jan Huss, "*Pravda vitezi*" (Truth shall prevail), which became the motto of the first president of the new Czechoslovakia, Thomas Masaryk. It also had a musical connotation, because the Morse code for the letter V is . . . —, three dots and one dash. These were the opening bar of Beethoven's Fifth Symphony, which he had explained as "Fate knocking at the door." It was easy to tap on door and window, and was henceforth to symbolize fate knocking at the door of the Third Reich.

Although at first scorned and ignored by the Germans, the V campaign was soon infuriating, and finally haunting, them. They ordered shopkeepers and householders whose walls and windows were marked to obliterate the V sign, or be held responsible for it. It was displayed not only on these surfaces, but in other more unusual ways. In the Paris metro, people alighting tore their tickets into the shape of Vs and threw them down, so that the metro floors everywhere became *Champs de Victoire*. After failing to outlaw the practice, the Germans decided in desperation to adopt it themselves, to appropriate the V as a symbol of German victory. They announced that *Viktoria* was an old, perfectly good, Teutonic-Latin word for victory, which had only been replaced by *Sieg* in relatively modern times. In June 1941, therefore, they began to use posters in the occupied zone of France bearing a huge white V beneath which was a pendant swastika. Below this was written, "*Viktoria*—the victory of Germany which is fighting for the New Europe." They even painted the V on their own vehicles. The most prominent of these plagiarized signs was on the Eiffel Tower, and on the pediment of the Chambre des Députés, on the front facing the Pont de la Concorde. Here, two gigantic Vs forty feet high were erected, with the motto beneath, "*Deutschland siegt an allen Fronten.*" This German use of the V continued throughout the occupation, until in the summer of 1944 they began to use the letter for another purpose—the V-1 and V-2 (*Vergeltung*—vengeance) rockets which fell on London.

The Nazis tried to turn the "V" campaign to their own use. (Top) A German poster, "V—Germany victorious on all fronts." (Second row, left and right) The V in occupied Holland. (Third row) The Germans equated the V with the Latin word victoria. (Bottom row) An anti-Semitic leaflet. (Opposite page, top left) A German poster issued in connection with the 1941 Allied collapse in Greece. (Top, right) The German long-range rockets were called V-1 and V-2. (Bottom, left) A Dutch postcard published by the Germans. (Bottom, right) A Nazi propaganda postcard.

Unlike the Germans, the various resistance movements could not use the poster as a form of propaganda; it was too dangerous to put up. But they could deface German posters. Never before, it was said, had Paris known such a plague of posters. Tearing them down was a punishable offense. A man who tore down a caricature of Winston Churchill as an octopus was given a three-month sentence and a heavy fine. Much quicker, and less dangerous, was to scrawl the V sign on the German poster.

The propaganda material employed by the resistances came largely from British and American sources. Not long after the evacuation of Dunkirk, the RAF was already dropping leaflets on the French, informing them that the British would come back.

The Allies took some time to realize that the propaganda they provided had to be adapted to the psychology of the occupied country in question. Before attempting to influence public opinion, care had to be taken not to offend it. In unoccupied France, for instance, in 1940 and 1941, it would have been impolitic to defame Marshal Pétain, whose popularity was then at its height. It proved more rewarding to attack his subordinates, in particular Pierre Laval, or at the most to refer sympathetically to the baneful effects of old age on human judgment.

Nazi propaganda in the experienced hands of Dr. Goebbels was by 1941 presenting the war as a grand crusade to save Europe and the world from Bolshevism. The Allies had to counter this logically, explaining why they were now joined with the Soviet Union in the struggle. This they did by quoting Winston Churchill, who had said he would make a pact with the devil to destroy such an evil thing as Hitlerism.

As the war progessed, the Allies also learned that the military situation must be reported accurately to the occupied countries, without concealing Allied reverses. In any case, these reverses would be given full publicity by the Nazis. To anticipate their announcement was a sure sign of confidence and self-assurance. Unlike the Nazis, whose propaganda was broadly addressed to the lowest human denominator—as Goebbels himself boasted— the Allies appealed to reason and the critical sense of their European audience. In the early stages they made many mistakes. During the fighting in Norway in April 1940, the BBC made extravagant claims for Allied successes, which only made the Norwegians disillusioned with the West when the Germans occupied the entire country. Here the British prime minister, Neville Chamberlain, did not help matters with his confident "Hitler has missed the bus" speech. As late as August 1944, the BBC made a premature announcement about the fall of Paris, which might have been costly and bloody for the jubilant Parisians. On the whole however the influence of Allied propaganda, principally the BBC and the American leaflet campaigns, in the occupied territories was to uplift morale and to inspire the inhabitants to greater feats themselves. This was confirmed in thousands of letters from listeners which came through Spain and Portugal, or from those who had escaped. From Bergen to the Basque country, from Amsterdam to Athens, every evening in thousands of homes and shops, the shutters would be closed

Pierre Laval as seen by the American cartoonist, Daniel Fitzpatrick, (Top) and the Russian artists, the Kukriniksi (Bottom). Though Marshal Pétain became chief of the French State after the Germans occupied France in 1940, Laval, by 1942, emerged as the virtual dictator of the Vichy regime. Following the liberation, he was sentenced to death and executed.

early, the lights extinguished and the inhabitants would gather in silence round the radio, straining to catch the muffled tones of London.

Charles de Gaulle, leader of the "Free French" in exile, frequently broadcast to his countrymen, urging them to resist until the Allies arrived; and the daily broadcasts of Queen Wilhelmina from London were a ray of hope to the Dutch, who accepted her as the symbol of national independence and survival.

When America was still neutral, her short-wave broadcasts to occupied Europe were often more effective than the BBC emissions. Many Europeans felt that a neutral country was more likely to tell the truth than was a belligerent. Moreover, the American broadcasts revealed where American sympathies lay, although she was neutral; and this in turn persuaded the people in 1940 and 1941 that, in spite of all appearances to the contrary, Britain's chances of winning must be good. Penalties for listening to these foreign broadcasts increased as the war continued. In 1943 the Nazis began confiscating radio sets in Holland. But people handed in only their old, broken-down sets and kept the good ones. At the end of the war, 20 percent of the sets, it was estimated, were still concealed and listened to at night.

Early in the occupation, a clandestine press appeared, the fruit of spontaneous efforts by the occupied peoples themselves. Editing was relatively easy—with material obtained chiefly from American and BBC broadcasts and leaflets—but printing and distribution, the shortage of paper and equipment, and the stringent security measures which had to be applied, presented exceptional problems. A rotary press was difficult to acquire, and the essential collaboration of professional printers could not be relied upon. In Poland, small hand presses were set up in the cellars of townhouses or, if they were too noisy, in shacks in the woods. News from all over the world was collected by radio monitors concealed in soundproof cellars, forest huts, and barns with false roofs. Farmers' carts brought paper to the printers, concealed under loads of hay or vegetables. Distribution was on the "threesome system," each distributor knowing only the person who handed him the paper and the one he passed it on to. The news sheets were also distributed through shops, concealed in goods, or sometimes sold openly from street kiosks, hidden inside the pages of German newspapers.

In Belgium, two clandestine papers appeared as early as June 15, 1940: *Chut (Buffoon)* in Brussels and *Le Monde du Travail (Working World)* in Liège. A month later, history repeated itself when *La Libre Belgique (Free Belgium)* appeared, to carry on the clandestine tradition of its famous namesake under the 1914–18 occupation. Its articles were remarkably outspoken. On August 15, 1941, an unusual anniversary, it wrote:

After overrunning Belgium and France, the Führer said that by August 15, 1940 he would be reviewing a parade of his troops in London. His astrologers and pythonesses had told him! But he lost the air battle over London, and now. . . . the Boche marches furiously up and down the channel coast looking out impotently on the twenty-three miles of water which separates him from what Hitler thought would be an easy prey. . . . Because of a shortage of metal, Hitler then attacked Russia. . . . now the RAF is nightly giving him more metal than he wants. . . .

When the Nazis took over the principal Brussels newspaper *Le Soir*, the Belgians immediately rechristened it *Le Soir Volé* (*Le Soir*, stolen). On November 9, 1943, thousands of copies of a fake *Le Soir* were delivered by bicyclists to all the Brussels kiosks, an exact imitation of the paper under German control, containing nothing but anti-German propaganda. Just before the liberation in 1944, 275 clandestine newspapers, many in Flemish as well as French, were being published in Belgium.

In Holland on May 15, 1940—two days after the capitulation —a Haarlem tapestry maker launched the first clandestine news sheet, *Action de la Gueux* (*Beggar's Action*). By 1941, 120 clandestine news sheets were circulating in the country. Much the same could be said for Denmark and Poland. In France, the Résistance newspapers bore significant names—*Combat, Libération, Franc-Tireur, Valmy*, etc. In Paris Emilien Amanauny founded "Le groupe de la rue de Lille," an organization which provided Résistance papers with news and other press facilities. It was never discovered by the Gestapo. By 1944, over a million copies of the clandestine press were circulating in France.

All these newspapers and sheets specialized in detailed accounts of what the people could not otherwise know, particularly the German military setbacks. Among other regular themes was "how the Germans are plundering our food supplies"—most apposite and widely read in a period of acute food shortage. There were, in fact, a number of other reasons for the food shortage, including the Allied blockade, but only "the German occupation" was given. Some clandestine news sheets were even addressed directly to the soldiers of the Wehrmacht, to awaken their *Heimweh*, or longing to return home to a normal existence with their families, and to remind them constantly of the dangers their families were now exposed to by the Allied bombing. Foreign units incorporated in the Wehrmacht were also canvassed; ethnic Germans from Poland, Slovakia, Transylvania, and the Ukraine. What were they doing here, so far from home, waiting to be killed by the Anglo-Saxons on behalf of Hitler? Another regular press feature was the action of the resistance, details of trains derailed, bridges blown up, factory stoppages, all aimed at encouraging emulation. The news sheets also informed people how to hoard those metals necessary for the German war effort, such as copper and nickel, how to sabotage machinery and how, for the younger and more active, to kill with the hands.

The use of the cinema for resistance purposes was severely limited. Most French directors, prevented by the censorship of scripts from supporting it openly, could only indulge in elaborate fantasy, or historical films in which an intelligent audience might see a parallel with the present. Such a film was *Pontcarvel*, about the 1815 Restoration of the Bourbons. It was full of double entendres about the Vichy regime, which escaped the censor and delighted the French audiences. The hero, Colonel

In all occupied countries, the underground press served as a lifeline for resistance groups. Two Belgian clandestine newssheets were L'alouette *(Top) and* La Meuse *(Bottom). These papers were crudely reproduced. They contained news gleaned from short-wave broadcasts, editorials, and poetry. In France, several clandestine journals had circulations of more than 10,000.*

(Top) A poster for a Franco-American festival in Paris after the liberation. (Middle and bottom, right) Two scenes from Rene Clement's Bataille du Rail (Battle of the Rails, 1945). The film described the sabotage of the French railroads by the resistance during the German occupation. (Bottom) A French poster by Raymond Gid commemorating those missing during the war.

THÉATRE NATIONAL DE L'OPÉRA • 24 JUILLET 1945

PACIFIQUE 45

APRÈS BERLIN...TOKYO !
FESTIVAL FRANCO-AMÉRICAIN

SEMAINE DE L'ABSENT
24 DÉCEMBRE-1ᵉʳ JANVIER

Pontcarvel of the Empire, barricades himself in his house and fights off the reactionary troops. He became a symbol of the Résistance, one of whose military leaders took the name Pontcarvel. In *Les Visiteurs du Soir*, the film makers returned to the Middle Ages, the time of the devil and his sorcerers. On the one hand are the good beings, those sanctified by love; on the other, the evil ones led by the devil. Originally the script writers intended the devil to be a portrait of Adolf Hitler, but this allusion could not be fully realized without too great risks. However the point was clear. In the last scene, the devil turns the young lovers into stone but—so runs the fantasy—they are only united in love in the stone statue, and their hearts beat there in unison . . . an image of petrified France itself. Evil is powerless to conquer love and goodness.

In Denmark a similar effect was obtained in a documentary made by the Danish Agricultural Pests Commission. This was about an insect plague, the *sitophilus granariae*, which destroys the crops. Passed by the German censor on nutritional grounds, it was shown throughout the war to Danish audiences who fully appreciated the satire. Everyone knew what the last line meant: "Remember that Danish crops are at stake."

Ironically, the success of the resistance propaganda was due principally to its use of the very weapons which Goebbels had perfected in the 1930s. The radio with which he had indoctrinated the Germans and terrified half of Europe with Hitler's threatening speeches, boomeranged against him during the war from the stations of the BBC. Without their constant broadcasts, high morale could not have been maintained in the occupied territories, nor could instructions for sabotage have been so easily conveyed. Without the airplane, with which Germany had rocked the continent in 1940 and 1941, no leaflets could have been dropped. Without modern printing, hundreds of clandestine newspapers could not have been read. When Winston Churchill wrote that the Nazis had conquered half of Europe, benefitting "from the lights of perverted science," he was referring to the destructive uses to which they had put these new propaganda weapons. However, as Goebbels was to learn, they proved also to be very two-edged weapons.

"The true face of Rexism," 1939/Belgium/
René Magritte.

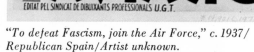

"To defeat Fascism, join the Air Force," c. 1937/
Republican Spain/Artist unknown.

"Unification," c. 1937/
Republican Spain/Artist unknown.

Anti-Italian poster, c. 1937/
Republican Spain/Artist unknown.

(Top, right) Commemorative for the 2nd anniversary of
the Defense of Madrid, November 7, 1938/Republican
Spain/Artist unknown. (Bottom) Commemoration of the
150th anniversary of the U.S. Constitution, June 1, 1938/
Republican Spain/Artist unknown.

Marshal Petain issue, 1941/
France, Vichy government/J. Piel.

"Men of France," no date/France, Vichy
government/Artist unknown.

"The women and children of Europe accuse the RAF,"
1940/German poster for France/Theo Matejko.

"Thanks to the British, our cross we bear," 1940/
German poster for France/signed SPK.

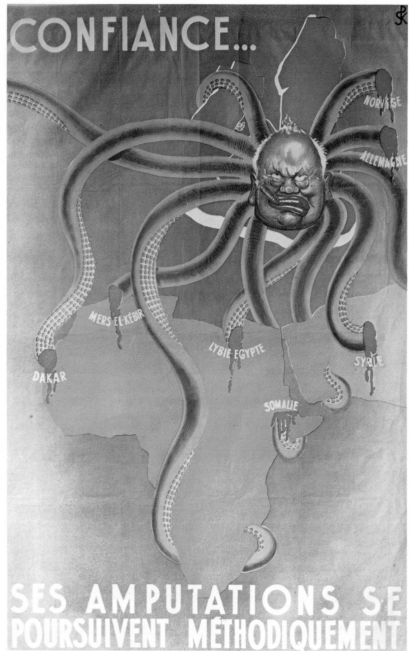

"His amputations continue systematically,"
no date/German poster for France/signed SPK.

"They give their blood, give your work." Give your work
to save Europe from Bolshevism, c. 1942/German poster
for France/Artist unknown.

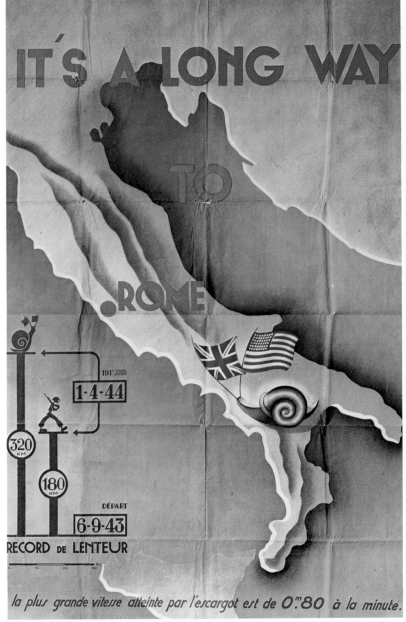

"The Allies are advancing at a snail's pace,"
1944/German poster for France/Artist unknown.

"Europe united against Bolshevism," c. 1943/
German poster for France/Artist unknown.

*"Black market, crime against the community," 1943/
France, occupation government/Ph. H. Noyer.*

"And you? Become a W.A. Man," no date/
Holland, occupation government/Lou Manche.

"Dutchmen, fight Bolshevism in the Waffen SS,"
c. 1943/German poster for Holland/Artist unknown.

"Bolshevism is murder," no date/
German poster for Holland/Artist unknown.

"Moscow commands," no date/German poster
for Holland/Artist unknown.

"Prove you're a true Dutchman, join the Waffen SS,"
c. 1943/German poster for Holland/Artist unknown.

"The 'liberators' will save European culture from its downfall,"
1944/German poster for Holland/Leest Storm.

"*All is well, Madame la Marquise . . . ,*" *no date/*
Belgium, occupation government/Artist unknown.

"*Join the National Socialist Transport Corps,*"
no date/German poster for Belgium/Wieland.

"*Europe is prepared. Join the Flanders Legion,*"
c. 1943/German poster for Belgium/Claudius.

"*Waffen SS Recruitment Command,*" *c. 1943/*
German poster for Belgium/Bertau.

"Danger threatens from the sky. Take air raid precautions," 1938/Finland/T. Kivihariu.

Published by the Free French Movement in
America, no date/USA/Jean Carlu.

Published by the Free French Movement in
America, no date/USA/Henri Laussucq.

Published by the Belgian Information Center,
no date/USA/R. Sturbelle.

Published by the Belgian Information Center,
c. 1944/USA/V. Rotter.

The Danish church as a symbol of resistance,
no date/USA/Artist unknown.

Published by the Czechoslovak Information
Service, no date/USA/Adolf Hoffmeister.

Published by the Greek War Relief Association,
no date/USA/Artist unknown.

A vision of the Yugoslav spirit, no date/USA/
Vladimir Ivanovic.

*Anti-German postcards, 1945/Holland/Nico
Broekman and Smits.*

Anti-German postcard, 1944/Belgium/
Artist unknown.

THE SOVIET UNION PROPAGANDA FOR PEACE 1917–1945

We think it will not be much longer
before Alexander Nevsky will be
shown in public theatres again.

SERGEI EISENSTEIN
to Margaret Bourke White,
shortly before the
German invasion in June 1941.

One feature which the Soviet and Nazi regimes had in common before the Second World War was their regard for the technical inventions of the 20th century—the radio, the cinema, the popular press (as well as automobiles, airplanes, and wireless telegraphy). These were seen by the two regimes as a means of dominating their fellow men. Whereas in the Western democracies in those years, the communications media were mostly in private hands, for entertainment and commercial gain, in the Soviet Union and Germany they were state monopolies, used primarily for disseminating propaganda.

Other similarities in the propaganda systems of the two countries are well enough known: the indoctrination of youth at an early age; the constant repetition of slogans and catchwords; the diatribes against the bourgeois "plutocracies;" the censorship of all news from abroad; the sudden switches of government policy. In one aspect of propaganda, however, there was an important difference.

Whereas the Nazis, as well as Mussolini's Fascists, presented themselves essentially as warriors, and attempted by a continuous show of force—military parades, rallies, and bellicose speeches—to terrify the rest of Europe into submission (e.g. the effect of the Nazi film *Baptism of Fire* on Norway and the Low Countries in 1940), the Soviets always posed as men of peace. Hitler and Mussolini were forever strutting about in uniform; but the Russian leaders, on the few occasions when they showed themselves outside the Kremlin, appeared dressed in their neat dark suits and Trilby hats, the personification of civilian propriety. Indeed, the Soviets' appropriation of the word "peace" is one of the most remarkable propaganda achievements of our time. They took possession of it completely, arrogated it as it were to their exclusive use.

A glance at the names of some of their front organizations in the United States alone reveals this: The American Committee for the Struggle against War, The American League against War and Fascism, and The World Congress against War, to mention only a few. For the average Western citizen not much interested in politics, but aware of the horrors of modern warfare, this all sounded much more attractive than the martial rodomontades of Hitler and Mussolini.

Where the propaganda machinery is state controlled, it is easy to account for contradictions in meaning by the use of a special vocabulary. To most people, for example, the Soviet invasion of Finland in 1940 was "war." But to the Soviet propagandists it was "A rectification of frontiers to protect the pacific Soviet state against an attack by the Western Imperialist warmongers."

Long before Goebbels appeared on the scene, the Communists were fully alive to the importance of propaganda. Already in 1902 Lenin, in his book *What Is to Be Done?*, had expatiated on its revolutionary value. By 1910 his lieutenant in Baku, Joseph Stalin, was running a full-scale propaganda bureau, financed from the proceeds of bank raids. With the triumph of the October Revolution in 1917, they set up the Department of Agitation

(Below) Until the end of 1933, the Soviets maintained friendly relations with Nazi Germany. Though Hitler had annihilated the Communists in Germany, the Soviets felt less threatened. They saw Nazism as a desperate attempt to stave off the inevitable proletarian revolution in Germany and expected it to fail. After the signing of the German-Polish Nonaggression Pact in January 1934, the Soviets shifted their stand, suspecting that Germany would help Poland to seize parts of the Ukraine. From 1934 until the signing of the Nazi-Soviet Nonaggression Pact in August 1938, Soviet propaganda, such as this 1936 cartoon by Boris Efimov, attacked Hitler and the Nazi Party.

ON A SHAKEY THRONE.

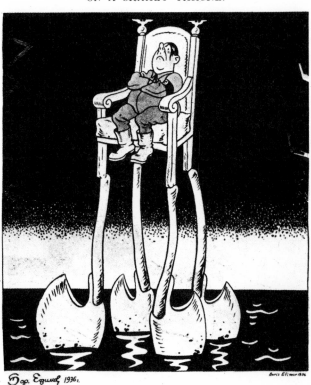

(Below) Sergei Eisenstein directing the Battle on the Ice sequence for Alexander Nevsky *(1938). The tension in this sequence was heightened by the closely coordinated score of Sergei Prokofiev. The film, which dramatized the Russian victory over the Teutonic Knights near Novgorod in the 13th century, was a thinly veiled challenge to Hitler's* Drang nach Osten. *(Opposite page, top) Nicolai Cherkasov as Nevsky. Cherkasov closed the film with a patriotic declaration spoken directly to the audience. "Whosoever comes against us by the sword shall perish by the sword. Such is the law of the Russian land and such it will always be." (Opposite page, below) The soldiers of Novgorod massing for the battle against the Teutons on ice-covered Lake Peipus. Following the Stalin-Hitler Pact,* Alexander Nevsky *was removed from circulation until the Germans invaded the Soviet Union in 1941.*

and Propaganda in Moscow, which took complete control of all information media. In *What Is to Be Done?* Lenin had made an interesting distinction between the two concepts, agitation and propaganda. "Agitation," he wrote, "is for the ignorant masses, presenting them with a single, simple idea which by constant repetition will be rammed home. The propagandist, on the other hand, deals with more complex issues and ideas—so many that they can be understood only by a few people." The agitator therefore, according to Lenin, was inclined to the spoken word, the propagandist to the written. In another book, *The Rape of the Masses*, the writer Serge Chakotin made much the same distinction about the Russians; he divided them into two categories, the 10 percent who were the active minority, and the 90 percent who formed the dull, brute mass. For the masses, propaganda had to be simple, categoric, direct.

Within a short time all forms of printing—books, newspapers, pamphlets, and posters—were in the hands of the State Publicity Corporation, which controlled not only the publishing operations but the printing machinery and paper supply. It was endowed with a censorship department which examined all book manuscripts, film scripts, drawings, music, and even maps. On November 12, 1920, the Main Political Education Committee of the Republic was set up, branches of which were attached to the political division of every region, district, town, and village.

Widespread illiteracy was the immediate problem, and it was here that the recently invented radio and cinema came to the rescue. In rural districts, radio receivers were placed in communal "reading huts," clubs, dormitories, houses of culture, museums, parks, and other public institutions where the peasants were encouraged to congregate and listen. In the reading huts they were exposed to posters as well as radio broadcasts. The huts were rudely built and generally had earthen floors. The peasant would have to come to them for information about the food situation and rationing, local notices, etc.; while there, he would also receive a broadside from the radio about the iniquities of the old Czarist system, and the benefits of the new Bolshevik one.

For the illiterate in those early days, the wall poster also proved invaluable. While the Civil War was still in progress, the windows of the press agency, Rost, in every town and village were plastered with brilliantly colored posters by such well known artists as Mayakovsky, depicting the triumphs of the Red Army. Illustrated wall newspapers were also used to give a simplified account of the Five Year Plan.

The Communists were equally quick to make use of the cinema for the illiterate. They were innovators in the documentary field and their films had a strong element of persuasion. *Turksib*, for example, discarded the narrative and human aspect, in favor of a plea for the building of the Turkestan-Siberian railway. Other topical themes were taken from the Five Year Plan, to persuade workers and peasants that no sacrifice could be too great to achieve its goals.

When it became clear in the 1930s that Germany would be

(Below) Sergei Mezhinsky as a Jewish surgeon persecuted by the Nazis in Professor Mamlock *(1938), directed by Adolf Minkin and Herbert Rappoport. One of the strongest anti-Nazi films made before the war,* Professor Mamlock *was also used as propaganda in the United States and England shortly after its completion. Mamlock is humiliated solely because he is Jewish and finally shot for offering open resistance to the Nazis. (Opposite page, top) A scene from Grigori Roshal's* The Oppenheim Family *(1939), another strong anti-Nazi film released at the height of the tension just before the Nonaggression Pact. The film was adapted from a 1933 novel by the Jewish writer Lionel Feuchtwanger; its theme, the persecution of a Jewish family. (Opposite page, below) Another scene from* Professor Mamlock. *The Jewish surgeon is paraded through the streets and scorned by Nazi sympatherizers.*

the enemy in any future war, a number of films were made to prepare the public. The great director Sergei Eisenstein was commissioned to do a film about Alexander Nevsky, the 13th-century Russian hero and conqueror of the Teutonic Knights who had invaded Russia in 1242. The implication was that what the Russians had done under Nevsky, they could do again under Stalin. *Alexander Nevsky* (1938) was immensely popular and was shown all over the Soviet Union. Eisenstein received Russia's highest award, the Order of Lenin. He was congratulated by Stalin, who had taken a personal interest in the filming. When the Soviets signed the nonaggression pact with Germany in 1939, the film was withdrawn from circulation—until the Nazi invasion of the Soviet Union in 1941. By a happy coincidence, Nevsky's defeat of the Teutons in 1242 took place at Lake Peipus near Leningrad, where the same humiliation was inflicted on their Nazi heirs in 1944. Other anti-Nazi films were *The Oppenheim Family* (1939), about Jewish pogroms and concentration camps in Germany, and *Professor Mamlock* (1938), about an eminent Jewish surgeon who opposed the Nazis. These too were withdrawn from circulation in 1939 and later rereleased after the German invasion.

In the early days after the revolution, when propaganda was in its infancy, the Bolsheviks, its first modern protagonists, made many mistakes. They were perceptive enough to see that religion, Lenin's "opium of the people," would be a powerful psychological enemy. In their determination to control people's minds, they decided that religion must be obliterated overnight. Here they overplayed their hand. Their "Union of the Militant Godless" organized a procession through the streets of Moscow of all the gods and prophets. It included Buddha on horseback in a state of priapic lubricity, the Virgin Mary lying on her back, also in a voluptuous posture, and a repulsive-looking Catholic priest making overtures to a beautiful maiden. In December 1922 in Leningrad, the Union of the Militant Godless erected a scaffold in the middle of the Nevsky Prospect, on which effigies of the gods, saints, popes, and prophets were ceremoniously beheaded and burned. In the Soviet press, the clergy of every faith were ceaselessly attacked for the alleged gluttony and drunkenness which accompanied their religious festivals. At Easter, a shop window in Moscow was decorated with a waxwork of six priests in a small boat swilling vodka, with quantities of empty bottles littered around them. This early period was also one of confiscation, and often willful destruction, of church property. The churches with everything they contained, such as sacred vessels, liturgical vestments, church bells, etc., were proclaimed national property and turned into warehouses, cinemas, and stables.

This sort of thing may have had some effect, but most of the workers and peasants—the new regime's main concern—were deeply shocked by this sacrilege. A leading Communist, Zarianov, complained about the indifferent results obtained from this anti-God propaganda. He said that when soldiers who had been subjected to it during their army service returned home,

(Top) Daniel Fitzpatrick's cartoon
from the St. Louis Post-Dispatch
showed Stalingrad as a death trap for
the German army. (Bottom)
Boris Efimov's comment on the
subservient German press, c. 1936.
After Hitler and Stalin signed the
Nonaggression Pact, German papers
were directed not to refer to ideological
differences between the two countries
and to use only "favorable comments
from friendly and neutral countries."

GATEWAY TO STALINGRAD
NOVEMBER 25, 1942

COUNTENANCE OF THE UNIFIED PRESS.

they were consulting the priests again within a couple of weeks, and paying them to say masses. He said that the "Anti-God Campaign" had been grossly mishandled. The 2,000-year reign of the church could not be effaced by crude stump oratory.

The Communists still intended to eradicate religion, which they described as "an evil no less pernicious than alcoholism or prostitution." But they now refrained from persecuting it directly, and adopted subtler methods. Ribald parodies of sacred themes and dignitaries were replaced by serious lectures, discussions, and seminars with scientific arguments. The process of fostering antagonism between religious sects and creeds was unobtrusively encouraged, and the priests were allowed to go about their daily business without being insulted.

Communist propaganda to foreign countries was always more subtle, based on the peace theme, and it took account of national character and temperament. The United States, in terms of communist ideology, was the most important country of all. Of it, Stalin said, "When a revolutionary crisis develops in America, that will be the beginning of the end of world capitalism as a whole."

When the American League for Peace and Democracy proclaimed, "Let us work towards the stopping of the manufacture and transport of munitions and other materials essential to the conduct of a Fascist war," many Americans could only applaud such a desirable aim. Nor was there much objection to the proclamation by the Communist Party of California, "Remember that the Soviet Union with 185,000,000 people is antiwar. Join in the defense of the peace policy of the only socialist country in the world, the Soviet Union."

In the 1920s, before Nazi Germany became the principal enemy, Soviet propaganda was directed largely against the powerful Western "plutocracies," and the horrors which their capitalist system had unleashed on the world between 1914 and 1918. The world was told that the capitalists would do it again, this time against the Soviet Union, because she was "the motherland of the international proletariat, and the only factor for its emancipation." The Communists even presented the coming war as desirable, because it would weaken capitalism more than communism. In the words of the 1928 Comintern Congress, it would "broaden the base of the proletarian movement everywhere, and bring nearer the world victory of Communism." This propaganda was broadcast on short-wave from the Soviet Union all over the world, in seventeen languages. The transmitter at Noginsk near Moscow was one of the most powerful in the world. In 1942, when Tito's partisans became active in Yugoslavia, the USSR set up a transmitter at Tiflis known as "Free Yugoslavia," purporting to be from within Yugoslavia. Later, it did the same for Bulgaria and Slovakia.

In the Soviet Union, as in Germany, Italy, and other countries where all communications media were centralized, an entire propaganda campaign could be changed overnight. On August 23, 1939, the Soviet Union and Germany, who had been insulting and threatening one another for years, signed a pact of friendship and nonaggression. It contained their agreement to the partition of Poland. A few days after its signature, on September 1, 1939, Germany invaded Poland and World War II began. Three weeks later, when Polish resistance was completely broken by the Germans, the Soviets also invaded. Yet the pact was explained in Moscow at the time as a "peace" measure, in these terms:

"The signing of the nonaggression pact between the USSR and Germany is not a war alliance between the two powers. It is not an agreement for the partition of Poland. . . . In this sense, the pact is the only real contribution to the security of Poland that has been made to date. In doing this, the Soviet Union had made a real contribution to an understanding of the present crisis in Europe. It has made a real contribution to the peace and security of Europe, the United States, and the world. . . ."

The war of 1939 brought immediate propaganda changes within the Soviet Union. Although still presenting itself as a "champion of peace," the Soviet Union now began to prepare its people for war. The armed forces were greatly expanded. A small but significant indication of this change was the issue of postage stamps depicting Soviet military power. Stamps now showed Red Army soldiers hurling grenades, and Soviet airplanes diving on enemy tanks. When in June 1941 the Germans attacked and the Soviet Union found itself allied with the Western democracies, postage stamps depicting the Big Three leaders in fraternal discussion, with the national flags of their countries intertwined above their heads, were issued. At the same time, the emphasis on the international nature of communism was reduced. The will to resist was encouraged in the Russian people by appeals to their patriotism rather than their communism; the war was described officially as "The Great Patriotic War." Films were made with such significant titles as *No Greater Love* and *In the Name of the Fatherland*. History was also rewritten to a certain extent; those czars who had distinguished themselves on the battlefield in the past were honored and held up as shining examples for the present. Stalin's frequent references in his speeches to Alexander Nevsky and Suvorov made everyone conscious of the link between the Russian past and present. An early wartime propaganda poster showing a Russian worker in combat with an aristocrat—probably inherited from Civil War times— was quickly withdrawn. The struggle now was national, not social.

The broad directives for propaganda came from the fountainhead itself, Stalin's orders of the day and his speeches on National Days. In his "Holy Russia" speech of November 6, 1941, the 24th anniversary of the revolution, he kindled national pride by recalling not only the great Russian generals of the past, but by associating them with great cultural figures like Pushkin, Tolstoy, Chekhov, and Tchaikovsky. The general line of propaganda was then determined by the Council of Peoples' Comisars and the Political Bureau of the All Union Communist Party. It was issued by the Propaganda Ministry to the country's many social and technical organizations—the Trade Unions

(Top) Soviet poster artists pulled no punches in depicting the Nazis as beasts and vermin. The text of this 1941 poster declares, "We'll destroy your teeth, hangman. We'll also cut your head with the red sword of retaliation." (Bottom) A 1941 Ukranian poster which proclaims "Destroy the Serpent." After initial setbacks, the Red Army fought valiantly to defend the Ukraine against Hitler's forces.

GOEBBELS ANTI-AIRCRAFT BATTERY

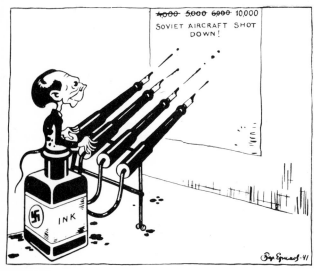

The Fascist Lie-Gun

Cooperatives, the Communist Youth Movement, the Union of Intellectuals, the Cinema Workers' Union, the Writers' Union, the Union of Workers in Art, to name only a fraction. All had special directives adapted to their particular needs.

The most effective means of conveying propaganda to the less literate—as the Soviet leaders had discovered twenty years before, during the Civil War—was the poster. The first of these, with the caption "We Shall Crush and Exterminate the Fascist Viper," appeared on the streets of Moscow the day after the German invasion. Within a few days, the editorial board of the "Tass Windows" had been formed and the Tass posters began to appear shortly thereafter. When Lord Beaverbrook visited the Soviet Union in 1941, he was so impressed by the Soviet posters that he asked Stalin for a collection to take home to England (where they were later exhibited). The tradition of Mayakovsky and the Civil War was revived by some of the best-known artists in wartime Russia—Sokolov-Skaya, Denisovsky, Lebedev, the Kukriniksi (a pseudonym derived from the names of three artists who worked as a team for twenty years—Mikhail Kuprianov, Porfiri Krylov, and Nikolai Sokolov). Many of the posters recalled the exploits of Russia's old national heros. In one, Alexander Nevsky, the victor over the Teutonic Knights in 1242, stood beside Suvorov, who defeated the Turks in the war of 1787; beside them, to bring it up to date, was Vasily Chapayev, who led a Bolshevik division against Kolchak's White forces in the Civil War. A parallel with the great Soviet counteroffensive of 1941–42 west of Moscow was suggested by a poster depicting General Kutuzov who, one hundred and thirty years before, had repelled another invader, Napoleon's army, before the gates of the capital.

In the gloomy days of 1941, the aim of these propagandists was to persuade the people that Mother Russia must finally prevail. Posters of huge Russian hands and steel pincers tightening on a German throat expressed the confidence which came with the first successful counterattacks. The posters often took the form of caricatures of the Nazi leaders; in particular Goebbels, who was depicted by Efimov in the satirical magazine *Krokodil* as Mickey Mouse with a swastika tail, and by Lebedev as a braying donkey. Pétain was shown placing France under the Nazi jackboot; and Hitler, dangling Hess on a fishing line as a bait to England to join the anti-Bolshevik crusade. A book of drawings by Sharmidov showed German war atrocities: looting, hanging mass burials.

These designs, rapidly produced by the stencil method, also acted as wall newspapers, announcing political and military successes. They could be as large as 10 feet high and half as broad, using fifteen to twenty different stencil colors. Some 200 artists in Moscow alone worked on these posters, which again, as in the Civil War, were displayed in the windows of the Tass press agency (formerly Rost) offices throughout the country. They were also distributed to every factory, farm, institute, hospital, army unit, and naval vessel, so that no Soviet citizen went untouched by them. They often included a pungent verse commentary by well-known poets like Marshak or Bedny, the children's book author.

The widespread popularity of war posters and cartoons in the Soviet Union was due to their simplicity and the talent of the Soviet artists who drew them, using a popular, comprehensible form of art. During the war this poster art went through several phases of development. The first posters, especially those by Moor, still showed certain influences of the Civil War posters. Abstract symbolic treatment of subjects, pronounced schematism of forms and limited color range (red, black, and white) were typical of this phase. Later war posters acquired new characteristics. This was largely explained by the fact that artists who had previously worked in easel painting or book illustration now tried their hand at posters. It was they who introduced heroic figures with emotional and psychological elements. Conventional decorative composition was replaced by realistic interpretation. The defeat of the Germans at Moscow, the gigantic battle of Stalingrad, the victorious advance of the Red Army, the liberation of Soviet territory, the fighting qualities and victories of the Allies were all reflected in the "Tass window" posters. There was not a single event in the war, in international or domestic affairs, which was not depicted in one Tass poster or another.

One exclusively Soviet wartime feature was the propaganda railway train. Its compartments were converted into printing presses and portable cinemas, and it was staffed with teams of lecturers, actors, and artists. They toured the country making speeches and supplying information about the war; they even penetrated into the battle zones, where the train stood in a siding camouflaged behind the lines.

The cinema also played an important role in the Soviet war effort. Within three days of the Nazi invasion, the first newsreels from the front were released. Thereafter, newsreel cameramen covered the war on all fronts; film projectors were installed in the big Moscow subway stations so that the public did not have to pay to see the commentaries. Films such as Eisenstein's anti-German *Alexander Nevsky* were resurrected; other films in the same patriotic vein, about Russian heros such as Kutuzov, were turned out. The barbarism of the Germans was depicted in *Zoya* (1944), about a real woman, Zoya Kosmodemyanskaya, a partisan who worked behind the German lines, where she was captured, tortured, and hanged. Another film about partisan activity, *Secretary of the District Committee*, was awarded the Stalin Prize for 1942. To depict the horrors of life inside Nazi Germany, Mikhail Romm's *Girl No. 217* (1944) told of an inhuman German family who had acquired a Russian slave girl.

The documentary studios were reorganized and famous directors employed. As speed was essential, the first documentaries were short, but by the end of the war they formed a complete chronical of its history—*The Defeat of the German Armies before Moscow* (1942), *Siege of Leningrad* (1942), *Battle for the Ukraine* (1943), *Battle of Orel* (1943), *Berlin* (1945), *Vienna* (1945). These documentaries described not only how the battles were won, but how they were planned.

(Below) In this 1941 cartoon by the Kukriniksi, a team of three Soviet artists, Goebbels tries to cover the fact that the Soviet air raid on Berlin took the Germans by surprise. Goebbels' greatest triumph as a speaker was his 1943 Sportpalast speech in Berlin where he managed to cover up the harsh facts of the German army's devastating defeat at Stalingrad and turn a total disaster into a cry for "total war." Germans joked about Goebbels' facile ability to churn out lies. (Following spread, left) The Kukriniksi ridiculed Goebbels' propaganda efforts which were no match for the Soviet air force. (Following spread, right) As the Russians piled up victories against Germany, Goebbels was portrayed as a desperate man rather than a comic figure.

LIE-LOCATORS

LES MENTEURS DE BERLIN

(Top) In 1942, when the Germans were on the offensive, cartoonists could only warn that the harshness of the Russian climate and terrain would defeat the Germans. (Bottom) The turning point was the victory at Stalingrad. Throughout the rest of 1943, propagandists like the Kukriniksi capitalized on a steady string of Soviet victories. (Opposite page) A more serious view of Hitler by the Kukriniksi.

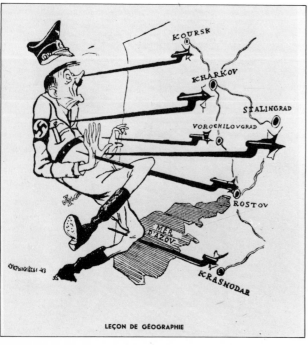

LEÇON DE GÉOGRAPHIE

To improve relations with the capitalist states, now the Soviet Union's allies, the Comintern was dissolved and the revolutionary "International" removed from the Soviet song book. In July 1941 Stalin, in order to make his regime appear more respectable in the eyes of the Christian world, did a political somersault. Up to and during the 1939–40 war, when the Soviets were invading eastern Poland, the Baltic states, parts of Finland, and Rumania, he had continued the atheist policy. The Union of the Godless under Jaroslavski had extended its activities to these conquered lands; 4,000 clerics of various confessions were deported from eastern Poland alone before mid-1940, and replaced by 25,000 antireligious agitators. But all this was changed overnight. One of Stalin's first acts after the German invasion in June 1941 was to announce the death of Jaroslavski (not, it later transpired, from natural causes). Stalin even told the Polish-American priest, Stanislas Orlemanski, that he would like to "collaborate with the pope against the coercion and persecution of the Catholic Church in Germany," adding that he was "a champion of freedom of conscience and religion." A Soviet Deparment of Church Affairs was set up in Moscow, its function being "to organize friendly relations between the government and the confessions." At this fearful moment with the Germans at the gates of Moscow, the Soviets were prepared to canvas support from every conceivable quarter. They even permitted the Polish forces under General Anders to have their own army chaplains; some fifty Polish Catholic chaplains who had disappeared into Soviet concentration camps in 1939 were released for this purpose. In Moscow, the French church was reopened and placed at the disposal of the Polish Catholic community.

In its propaganda to the Germans, the Soviet Union took a different line from that adopted by the Western Allies, who had decided at Casablanca in 1942 on the policy of unconditional surrender. They made no distinction between Hitler and any alternative German government, should the Nazis be overthrown internally. The Soviets however distinguished very carefully between the German people and their Nazi leaders, the "Hitlerites" as they were contemptuously called. In their broadcasts to Germany, the Soviets said they would have no truck with the Hitlerites, but with the people of Germany, the workers whom they assumed must be on their side, they had no quarrel. Stalin's statement, "The German state passes—the German people remain," summed up the Soviet attitude.

Soviet propaganda to the German prisoners of war—of whom there were tens of thousands after the Stalingrad victory—was aimed primarily at persuading them to turn against the men who had misled them. Playing on professional pride, they even persuaded a group of German generals, by showing them that Hitler was ruining the Eastern campaign with his bungling, amateurish methods, to lead a "Free German" movement against him. They had so many prisoners that the German General Staff could not keep track of the dead and wounded, whom they posted simply as "missing." The only way that German families could find out if their men were still alive was by listening to the Soviet radio

КУКРЫНИКСЫ 43.

*(Top) A poster by Dementry Shmarinov
declares "Revenge." In 1942, while the
Germans overran vast areas of Russia,
propagandists had to arouse the spirit
of vengeance in the Soviet people
with images such as this mother holding
her dead child. (Bottom) When victory
was close at hand, poster artists lost
no time in proclaiming the strength of
the Red Army.*

programs beamed to Germany, in which from time to time lists with names of German prisoners of war were read. The radio would announce that a prisoner was to be brought to the microphone, so that his relations could hear his voice. Time was given for the next-of-kin to be called to the radio; so that while waiting, the German relations had to listen to political and military talks of indeterminate length describing the German catastrophes and Allied victories. The Russian announcer would then address himself to the prisoner's next-of-kin: "Frau A. of Munich, your husband is here in the studio. He was taken prisoner near Rostov. He lost an arm but, as you will hear from his own lips, he is receiving good medical care and he will recover. You are lucky, Frau A. When the Hitlerites have been destroyed, you will see your husband again. But millions of other German wives and mothers are not so lucky. Their husbands and sons will not return. The criminal ambition of the Hitlerites has cost them their lives." Or the announcer would sometimes say, "Herr Z., here is your son. He was wounded and captured on the road to Bobruisk. Herr Z., what was your son doing on that wintry, snowy road to Bobruisk, so deep in Russia?"

The Russians were fortunate in one respect, thanks to the extraordinary psychological purblindness of the Germans in dealing with the occupied Eastern territories. In the Ukraine and White Russia, they had the most promising opportunity, for many people were violently anti-Soviet and welcomed them with open arms as "liberators." Yet Goebbels' great propaganda machine hardly went into action, nor indeed did it in all the Russian territory conquered in 1941 and 1942. No Ukrainian or Russian Ferdonnet broadcast to his people exploiting the weaknesses and shortcomings of the Communist party, or playing on the differences between the Russian people and their leaders. The reason was quite simple. The Nazis regarded the Slavs as illiterate subhumans on whom propaganda was wasted. They were to be beaten into submission by sheer brute force. Had the Nazis approached the Ukrainians with more subtle methods, the result might have been different. But the propaganda opportunity was not taken and the Nazis remained prisoners of their racial arrogance.

The Soviet Union's wartime propaganda, both abroad and to their own people, was remarkably successful. Abroad the Soviets could play on the sympathies of the British and Americans as allies sharing the same tribulations and the same hatred for a common enemy. They posed as liberators who would, after the victory, vacate the countries they had liberated in Eastern Europe. In a speech on November 6, 1941, Stalin had said: "Our cry is —No intervention of any kind in the internal affairs of other peoples! The equality of nations! The inviolability of territory!"

At home the propagandists had the advantage of dealing with a people accustomed after twenty years of communism to Draconian discipline and innumerable political volte-faces. This discipline, and the appeal to the people's deep-seated feeling for their homeland, enabled Stalin to mount a more successful military campaign than Hitler could ever have imagined.

"The proletarian counterattack will destroy the
fascist beast, 1930/USSR/Viktor Deni.

Meeting over Berlin, c. 1941/
USSR/Kukriniksi.

"Kill the fascist beast," 1942/
USSR/Viktor Deni.

"Remove your hat" says the fascist; "Off with your head"
is the partisan's response, 1941/USSR/Kukriniksi.

Pincers within pincers, c. 1942/
USSR/Kukriniksi.

REPRODUCED FROM SOVIET WAR POSTER 1941 · BY RUSSIAN WAR RELIEF INC.

Goebbels as Mickey Mouse, 1941/USSR/
Boris Efimov.

"The Big Three will tie the enemy in knots," 1942/
USSR/Kukriniksi.

Weapons for the front from the Soviet women,
1942/USSR/Alexei Kokorekin.

"May the example of our predecessors inspire you
in this war," 1942/USSR/Viktor Ivanov and O. Burova.

*More weapons and ammunition to defeat the
enemy, 1942/USSR/Viktor Ivanov.*

*"The fascist pirate can't escape the Marine
Guards," c. 1942/USSR/Vialov.*

"Follow this worker's example. Produce more for the front,"
1942/USSR/Alexei Kokorekin.

ВИННИЦА

*Winniza, Jewish commisar, no date/German
poster for occupied USSR/Artist unknown.*

Poster proclaiming Russian atrocities, no date/
German poster for the Ukraine/Artist unknown.

Brat-Brata, no date/German poster for Eastern
Europe/Artist unknown.

"Fight vigorously, sons of Suvorov and Chapayev,
1941/USSR/Kukriniksi.

"The strength of our weapons is hurled against
the enemy," 1941/USSR/Mal'tsev.

Во имя Родины
ВПЕРЕД БОГАТЫРИ!

For the Motherland's Sake, Go Forward, Heroes

"For the Motherland's sake, go forward, heroes,"
c. 1942/USSR/I. Toidze.

Mother's Farewell to a Soldier Son ("Be a Hero!"),
1941/USSR/Artist unknown.

Issued to honor Soviet war heroes and commemorate
the 25th anniversary of the Young Communist League,
1942-1944/USSR/Artist unknown.

*Commemoratives of war medals. (Top) Patriotic War
Order; Order of Prince Alexander Nevsky. (Bottom)
Order of Field Marshall Suvorov; Order of Field
Marshall Kutuzov, 1944/USSR/Artist unknown.*

*(Top) Issued to honor Soviet war heroes. (Bottom)
Issued to commemorate the Day of the Nations United
Against Germany, June 14, 1944/USSR/Artist unknown.*

Donkeys and Goebbels make the same noises,
no date/USSR/Vladimir Lebedev.

*The East Front general seeks orders and Hitler
deliberates, 1944/USSR/Kukriniksi.*

ТОВАРИЩИ! НОВЫМИ ТРУДОВЫМИ ПОДВИГАМИ
ВЫ ПОМОЖЕТЕ НАМ
ВОДРУЗИТЬ НАД БЕРЛИНОМ ЗНАМЯ ПОБЕДЫ!

"Comrades! Your renewed efforts will help hoist
the victory flag over Berlin," 1944/USSR/Viktor Ivanov.

THE RISE AND FALL OF JAPAN 1931-1945

Let's refrain from all senseless
entertainments. Let's all do physical
exercises in the open air for at least
two hours a day. Let's all thank our
farmers at every meal, and see that
not a single grain is wasted.
JAPANESE WARTIME SLOGAN

At the beginning of this century Japan was regarded by the West with a kind of benevolent condescension. America's Commander Matthew Perry had brought to the Japanese in the mid-1850s the doubtful advantages of "Western civilization;" and another American naval officer, Lieutenant Pinkerton of Puccini's *Madama Butterfly,* had helped create in Western minds the image of "the land of the cherry blossom and the chrysanthemum." Of the other Western nations, Great Britain—impressed by Japan's conquering of the Russian colossus in 1904—had welcomed "the gallant little Jap" as an ally in World War I. Yet within a decade of the war's end this genial image had vanished almost without trace. "The gallant little Jap" had become in Western eyes "the Prussian of the East." How did it happen?

In 1900 when Japan was still emerging from her medieval cocoon she had, with her population of 50 million, offered a most profitable market for Western goods; one of the cheapest dumping grounds in the world for American and European manufacturers. But as soon as the last remnants of medievalism had been cast off, she became, within two decades, an industrial power in her own right. Thanks to a large and cheap labor force, she was soon usurping not only traditionally Western markets, but underselling the Western nations in their homelands.

During the depression of the early 1930s, the Americans and Europeans applied severe tariffs against Japanese products. Japan was therefore forced to look elsewhere for outlets. Her chief source of coal and iron was China; and it soon became clear that here, and in neighboring East Asia, she must secure the markets on which she could permanently rely. This was bound to bring her into conflict with the Western powers who had hitherto dominated the area politically and commercially. The favorable Western image of Japan began to change.

This process was accelerated by increased unpopularity in the West after Japan invaded China in September 1931, on the pretext that the Chinese had blown up a portion of the Japanese-owned Manchurian railway at Mukden. The destruction was, in fact, engineered by the Japanese army as an excuse to go to war. The invasion was greeted with almost universal hostility in America, which was beginning to regard Japan rather than any European power as her future potential enemy. Although Congress passed neutrality legislation and declared that the United States would remain aloof from the Sino-Japanese conflict, both American and British sympathies lay with China, whom these countries helped by building the Burma road for the supply of war material. On April 18, 1933, Japan warned that China was her preserve, and she showed her displeasure at Western criticism by leaving the League of Nations, and later the Naval Conference. It was clear that a confrontation of some kind with the West must sooner or later ensue.

China had to defend herself against a modern military power as best she could, on her own. Her propaganda in the rural areas, where illiteracy was general and where radio and press were almost unknown, relied almost entirely on the spoken, sung, or

(Top) The Kellogg-Briand Pact, signed by fifteen nations in August 1928, was an agreement to renounce war and to adhere to arbitration for settling international disputes. Japan broke the pact in 1932 when she occupied Manchuria. As this American cartoon from the early 1930s shows, the League of Nations was too weak to oppose her. (Bottom) A Chinese poster showing Japan as the greedy aggressor.

他的貪慾能滿足嗎

"YOU CAN'T APPEASE THAT APPETITE!" a copy of a Poster by Chang Ting. 8

*Posters supporting the Chinese
Nationalists. (Top, left) A poster for
Chiang Kai-shek, one of the Big Four
Allied leaders. (Top, right) A poster
expressing British solidarity with the
Chinese. (Bottom) A poster promoting
the Chinese air force. (Opposite page)
A Chinese woodcut poster. The text
reads "National Unity! Defense in
Depth to make China a fortress that will
destroy the enemy."*

acted word—for acting has always been much appreciated by the Chinese peasantry. The poster, too, was used by the Chiang Kai-shek government with great effect to mobilize the population for military service. Propaganda squads toured battle areas behind the troops, traveling in trucks with as many as fifty actors, musicians, or poster artists. In the event of a retreat, they plastered the walls with posters written in Japanese, pointing out that it was uncivilized of the Japanese to bomb fellow Asians, and that the Chinese were too civilized to undertake reprisals in kind. It was about all they could do, because the Chinese did not yet possess an air force capable of retaliation. Wherever printing and other methods of dissemination were not available, the *Pi Pao*, a hand-written wall newspaper, was employed. Consisting of brief articles, illustrations, poems, songs, and cartoons, it was pasted on the walls for the passer-by to see. It attacked the Japanese and celebrated events of national importance such as new treaties with the United States or Britain, or the suppression of the opium trade. In 1937 a "defense film organization" was created in British-occupied Hong Kong, consisting of several small companies making propaganda films cheaply and quickly in the Cantonese dialect.

The Japanese invaders, for their part, also used posters to convince the Chinese that the Europeans, in particular the Americans and the British, were their worst enemies. They dramatized all the evils of the opium trade, allegedly encouraged by these two Western powers for their own sordid commercial ends. Local actors were arrayed as caricatures of typical Westerners, with long wax noses and curly blond wigs.

Until the invasion of China, the Japanese had regarded propaganda with a certain disdain. They even refused to use the word, calling it "thought war." Tradition had taught them that they were a more "spiritual" people than the Westerners, that they lived in a divine land, and that their emperor was a direct descendant of the sun goddess. They had observed the uses to which propaganda had been put in World War I by the Europeans, and considered themselves above such deceits. As late as 1937, a Mr. S. Shiba summed it up in a letter to the *Japanese Times* in which he deplored Japan's inability to state her case to the world. "The Japanese," he wrote, "still think that thought war is incompatible with the true spirit of Japanese knighthood—that *bushido* and propaganda are poles apart."

But just as "Westernization" could not be avoided in industrial advance—otherwise the superior armaments of the West could not be matched—so Western psychological warfare had to be equaled as well. From the beginning of the Chinese campaign, the Japanese Foreign Office had been organizing unofficial propaganda in the form of tourist agencies, traveling lecturers, trade delegations and so on. A Bureau of Thought Supervision was founded by the Ministry of Education in 1932. The army and navy inaugurated their own press services. Attached to the prime minister's office was a Cabinet Information Bureau, whose function was to guide public opinion at home, and enlist sympathy for Japan abroad. The bureau had closely examined the

Japanese walls were plastered with posters to promote the war effort. (Top, left) A 1939 poster to encourage air travel. (Top, right) "People's Anti–Air Raid Exhibit." (Bottom) Tojo's face smiles from a wartime wall bulletin produced by the Matsushita Electric Company. (Opposite page) The ABC Weekly was an English-language propaganda sheet for the Co-Prosperity Sphere.

東條首相の算術
2+2=80

これは戦時日本の算術だ 然し一度に
は出來ない 毎日いろいろと工夫・研究
して難しい仕事に勇敢に取組んで行き
今日は 2+2=5 明日は 2+2=7 にする
これが 2+2=80 にする生産増強の鍵だ

松下電器産業株式會社

propaganda techniques of Britain and Germany in World War I, and now began imitating them. As the groupings of the "have" and "have not" nations in Europe began to form, Japan's natural allies became, inevitably, the self-proclaimed "have nots," the Fascist states. Taking a leaf from *Mein Kampf*, Japan proclaimed that she too was being starved of *Lebensraum*; that the Western imperialists were drowning her in her own home waters.

In many ways the Japanese leaders, although late starters, had an easier task in shaping public opinion than Goebbels had in Germany. The Prussian spirit of obedience, which Goebbels fostered so ardently, did not prevail throughout the Reich. But the Japanese were, in this spirit of obedience, all "Prussian." The average Japanese had been formed by centuries of strict conformity to a rigid code of values. Isolated from any non-Japanese habit of thought until the late 19th century, he had never known the democratic tradition, the liberal notions of participation in government, the rights of the individual, of free speech, and so on—of which the Germans, who had felt the Renaissance and had been through the Napoleonic wars, were at least aware. From early times, Japan had been governed by a small oligarchy imposing its will on a docile populace.

In 1924, the *Kokuhonsha* association was founded by Baron Miranuma, "to guide the people's ideologies and make known the *kokutai*"—which means roughly "the uniqueness of Japan in being governed by a ruler having spiritual origins." By the 1930s, it had become the most important association in Japan; and a text on *kokutai* was distributed by the Ministry of Education to all schools and universities. Much was also made of *Hakko Ichiu*, another patriotic catchword resurrected from the past. According to Japanese tradition, it was used by the first human emperor of Japan, Jimmu, to describe Japan's divine mission. The phrase, which means "to bring the eight corners of the earth under the same roof," gave a religious flavor to what was to be a blatantly expansionist policy. The whole world would become a happy family with Japan as paterfamilias guiding all the nations. In Japan, statecraft and practical politics had always been interwoven with religion. The intricate political game was played behind a religious screen.

By the mid-1930s the government of Japan, following this trend, had become an appendage of the armed forces. The generals had acquired both legislative and executive power, and formed an independent body answerable only to the throne. Henceforth, the Diet (Japan's parliament) played the same role as did Hitler's Reichstag, rubber-stamping government decrees. The miltary not only carried out policy, they formulated it. In 1935 General Sadao Araki became minister of education, a post later assumed, when war broke out, by the prime minister, General Tojo. In the military indoctrination of youth, the Japanese generals showed that they had little to learn from Hitler and Mussolini. Military penetration soon transformed the educational system into a reliable weapon in the new thought war. Children were taught that soldiers killed in battle waited on the gods at the Japanese Valhalla, Yasukundi, and that the war with

[The A B C Weekly] 大正四年二月八日第三種郵便物認可　第六十六巻第九號毎週一回月曜發行　定價二錢

THE ABC WEEKLY

Vol. 66　No. 9　Tokyo, Mon., March 4, 1940　(Edited by N. Imai)　Price 2 *sen*

 ARCH 10 is the Army Day.

The War Ministry has **issued** many **posters like the one** shown here.

It has also published 120,000 pamphlets to **remind** the people **of** the day.

*　*　*

A future **grand champion** sumo **wrestler** is in Fukuoka Prefecture.

He is K. Minematsu **by name.**

Though only 16-years old, he is already five feet, eight inches tall.

He **weighs** 150 pounds.

March 10 = the 10th of March (三月十日). **the Army Day** (陸軍紀念日). **the War Ministry** [mínistri] (陸軍省).
cf. {**the War Minister** (陸軍大臣).
has issued [iʃuːd] (發行した). **póster** (ポスター, ビラ). **like the one shown here** (こゝに示したものの様な).
cf. {I want to have **one** like that.
(それのやうなのが欲しい).
{It's not the **one** I lost.
(それは僕のなくしたのではない).
álso (亦). **has públished** (刊行した). **pamphlet** [pǽmflit] (パンフレット, 小册子). **to remind the people of the day** (國民に當時を想起せしめるために).
cf. {The picture **reminds** me **of** my childhood.
(その寫眞を見ると私の子供時代を想ひ出します).
{I beg to **remind** you **of** your promise.
(約束を御忘れない様に).

*　*　*

a future grand chámpion [tʃǽmpiən] (未來の横綱,

横綱の卵子). **sumo wrestler** [réslə] (相撲, 力士). **Prefecture** [prɪːfektʃə] (縣). **by name** (名は).
cf. {Do you know all the students **by name**?
(生徒の名を皆知つて居るか).
{No, but I know every one of them **by sight**.
(否, しかし顔は皆知つて居る).
Though only...... (まだ......だけれども). **already** (すでに). **is**......**tall** (身長が......だけある). **weigh** [wei] (體重がある). **pound** (封度).

〜〜〜〜〜〜〜〜〜〜〜〜
◁ **本文應用練習課題** ▷
〜〜〜〜〜〜〜〜〜〜〜〜

❶ このポスターや小册子は戰地 (the front) へ送られます.
❷ 僕も君の持つてるやうなのを買ひ度い.
❸ 陸軍省は上記の命令 (order) を發した.
❹ 彼の顔を見たら先日の約束を想ひ出した.
❺ Answer:—
1. How tall do you stand?
2. How much do you weigh?

*(Top) A leaflet proclaiming Asian
solidarity against the Anglo-Americans.
Japan saw her destiny as the leader
of a resurgent Asia. Though "Asia for
the Asians" was an omnipresent
propaganda slogan, the Japanese
occupation of other Asian countries
was often harsh and oppressive.
(Bottom) Japanese leaflet which falsely
declared that the United States was
prepared to negotiate peace with
Japan in 1942.*

EXTRA

The Yankees Tender The Olive Branch Singapore Neutral Zone?

Lisbon 14th.

News has been received here that America has proposed her separate peace negotiation to Nippon. The proposal was made on 14th January 1942.

President Roosevelt is of the view that Singapore ought to be declared a Neutral Zone.

The Nippon is considering this Peace Proposal.

China was just, and had the support of the gods. In every school, the morning's work began with a procession to the courtyard, where the Japanese flag was run up and the national anthem played. Every family was urged to start the day at the same hour with radio calisthenics. Army officers were attached to all higher education establishments, to give military training. Unauthorized absence by students from any training session was punishable, and three such absences could result in expulsion. The officers would walk into the lecture rooms unannounced and, if they felt so inclined, criticize the lecturer in front of the students. In the Jesuit university of Jochi, the teaching fathers were made to undergo military training alongside the students. Scholarships were granted not for intellectual achievement or hard work, but on how well the student satisfied the Japanese military ideal. History books were revised, until history teaching was transformed into a course of ethics and morals. Books on the divinity of the emperor and the duty of the citizen to place everything, including life, on the imperial altar, became compulsory reading in all high schools and colleges. Until 1939, university officials were still appointed by the respective faculties; after that date, by General Araki. When World War II broke out, special emphasis in all educational establishments was laid on "navigation, aviation, horsemanship, and mechanics."

The Japanese militarists had also learned from the Nazis that broadcasting can play an important part in the indoctrination of the young. Unlike the textbook, the radio responds immediately to daily events. In 1935, school broadcasting was established on a nationwide basis. A radio "Morning Address" to schools was given twice a month, in which contemporary events were authoritatively discussed. Typical titles of these talks were: "The Spirit of Loyalty, Filial Piety, Devotion, and Obedience"; "One Strength—the Japanese"; and "Why Our Military Forces Are Strong."

Of the written word—books and the press—control had already been taken in the early 1930s by the Board of Information. Writers were urged to join national service groups, which gave instruction on what themes to choose. The number of newspapers was reduced, allegedly because of paper shortage. The real reason was that press power was to be concentrated in the hands of the progovernment newspaper magnates. The 1,200 newspapers circulating in 1936 had, by 1940, been reduced to 900. Just before the outbreak of war in 1941, all newspapers were converted into "public utilities."

Japanese newspaper correspondents abroad were rigorously controled. They had to submit their dispatches through the local Japanese embassies, legations, and consulates, which eliminated any material considered unsuitable. On arrival in Tokyo, these dispatches underwent a further pruning by the military censor. By the time they reached the editor's desk, they were seldom more illuminating than the releases of the government press agency, Domei. This body, which was founded in 1936, had a near monopoly of foreign news; no paper could exist without its services (c.f. D.N.B. in Nazi Germany, and Stefani in Fascist Italy). Domei issued directives about what newspapers could print, what material they should emphasize, and what attenuate. Before the advent of Domei, two press agencies had existed in Japan, one Nippon Dempo in private hands, and another semi-official. Both were fused in Domei.

In wartime, all these forms of governmental control were greatly extended. In 1942, the National and Patriotic Association of Publicists was founded, with thousands of "writers, speakers, novelists, historians, and philosophers." When the war began to go badly for Japan, they were charged with a series of lectures throughout the country "to educate the people on the danger of defeatist thoughts." "Literary patriotic rallies" were organized to study a series of books dealing with "the extermination of the British and Americans." To purge the nation entirely of the debilitating influence of American jazz, the All Japanese Songsters' Association was founded, and such harmless tunes as "Dinah," and even "Auld Lang Syne," were forbidden. Huge meetings were held all over the country entitled "To crush America and Britain." After the radio and press, these monster rallies on Nazi lines proved to be one of the government's most effective propaganda weapons.

Also modeled on the Nazi example were various patriotic weeks, organized at regular intervals, to remind the Japanese people of their civic duties. "The Week for Good Commercial Morals and Shady Transactions Prevention" suggested that the black market was active; the "Week against Rudeness and Bad Manners," that war weariness had set in. There was also a regular "Anti-Espionage Week." Japan had always been extremely spy-conscious, and much domestic propaganda warned against disclosure of information to strangers. Posters were widely distributed to portray the famous monkey trio—Hear no Evil, See no Evil, Speak no Evil.

Propaganda against the Americans and British had of course started much earlier, in the late 1930s. The term "dangerous thoughts" was then coined for all notions of Western civilization which conflicted in any way with Japanese social institutions. The Anglo-Saxon nations were depicted in Nazi terms as a plutocracy run by Jews, a soulless, godless civilization whose only idols were "materialism, utilitarianism, and individualism" —in contrast to the Japanese "spiritual" values. Sometimes they were referred to as the "redheaded barbarians from the West." American civilization was shown as at once barbaric and decadent; statistics about racial oppression and the lynching of blacks in the United States were given great prominence. Hollywood's conventional portraits of gangsterism and crime were quoted as typical of everyday life in America. The British came in for much the same abuse in short-wave broadcasts to the peoples of southeast Asia. They were portrayed as tyrannizing the natives in Malaysia, Burma, India, and Hong Kong, who were urged to rise and throw off the British yoke under which they labored and suffered.

In contrast to this anti-Anglo-Saxon propaganda was the cam-

(Top) A Japanese anti-American leaflet for China. The text reads "American victory means enslavement and Chinese victory, peace and prosperity." (Bottom) A scowling Chiang Kai-shek watches smiling Chinese stream toward the fortress of the Japanese puppet government at Nanking. This leaflet promised starvation and death under Chiang's Chungking regime.

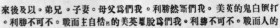

(Top) Five Scouts (1939), the first important Japanese war film, told the story of a group of Japanese soldiers caught in the middle of hostilities in northern China. (Bottom) Mud and Soldiers (1939) was another realistic wartime film. (Opposite page, top) A scene from The Flowering Port. (Opposite page, bottom) The Story of Tank Commander Nishizumi (1940) reflected prewar humanist ideals.

paign to glorify the Fascist powers, whose methods the Japanese militarists admired. After the signature of the anti-Comintern Pact with Germany, cultural exchanges on a wide scale between the two countries began. In December 1941, a German-Japanese cultural agreement was signed, and the *Reichsrundfunk* programs were broadcast to Japan by relay—and vice-versa for Japanese programs to Germany. These cultural exchanges did not always have the happiest results, particularly regarding the cinema. The Japanese realized, as did the Nazis, that for influencing the illiterate masses there was no better medium. The cinema enthusiast Goebbels persuaded the Japanese to collaborate in a joint celluloid venture to enshrine the unity of the Nazi group spirit with the racial spirit of the Japanese—to the detriment of the feeble and decadent spirit of the democracies. It was to be called *The New Earth*, and would be codirected by the German Arnold Fanck (Leni Riefenstahl's mentor) and Mansaka Itami, one of Japan's leading cineasts. Fanck wrote the script, which was about a renegade Japanese hero's conversion from democracy back to the faith of his fathers and the Japanese family creed. But Fanck did not—at least according to his colleague, Itami—understand the Japanese mentality sufficiently, and the script was so full of psychological errors that Itami insisted on reediting it. This infuriated the great Fanck, with the result that two versions of the film were produced: one for German, the other for Japanese consumption. Although *The New Earth* was a complete failure, Goebbels insisted on another joint production, *The Oath of the People*. This was an even bigger fiasco. After these two expensive attempts at collaboration, the Japanese turned to Asiatic partners for any joint film productions.

On the whole, the Japanese were good film makers; they had even in one short decade established a tradition of humanist films, such as *Five Scouts*. This was about the war in China, surprisingly free of Japanese nationalism and depicting in a completely objective manner the grim destiny of the soldier. But with the greater war approaching, their cineasts had to conform to a stringent code of instructions laid down by the Home Ministry. It prescribed "healthy entertainment value, with themes showing persons ready to serve patriotically." Subject matter included Japanese industrial and food production, and life in farming communities. After Pearl Harbor, the Japanese government encouraged warlike themes—known euphemistically as "national polity themes." The military leaders were very much impressed by the Nazi war films *Baptism of Fire* and *Victory in the West*. Japanese film makers were instructed to emphasize the spirit of complete sacrifice to the nation and the need to follow prescribed behavior regardless of difficulties. Individual success, love, or amusement were not to be emphasized. "Slice-of-life" films dealing with individual happiness, the life of the rich and idle, women smoking or drinking in cafes, and scenes of sexual frivolity were prohibited. One day of each month was set aside as free admission day to the cinemas for families with members doing their military service. On this

(Below) This Japanese leaflet shows the Philippines being rescued from the shoals of American imperialism and racial prejudice by the solidarity of her fellow Asians under Japan's leadership. The Japanese used such phrases as "the spiritual renovation of the Philippine people" while they marched thousands of Philippine soldiers to their death at Bataan. In 1938 Prince Konoe had proclaimed Japan's intention to establish a "New Order" which would insure the permanent stability of East Asia. After 1941, this doctrine was widely broadcast in Asia with the emphasis on Japan as the liberator. Though the Japanese granted the Philippines "independence" under quisling Jorge Vargas, it was for tactical reasons only.

day in every cinema and theater, one minute of meditation was required at midday to pray for those relations.

Apart from a spate of films about war heroics, with obvious titles such as *Torpedo Squadrons Move Out*, about three young officers sinking an American battleship (a film aimed at submarine recruitment), or *Falcon Fighters*, or *Volunteers of Death* about Pearl Harbor, there were one or two which were more subtle. *A Record of Love* aimed at inducing spinsters to marry disabled soldiers; it told of a woman who falls in love with a permanently disabled war hero, whom she marries and supports all her life by her own work. But there were few of these films. Most of them had the usual wartime propaganda themes; actresses being heroines in steel foundries or, as in *Most Beautifully*, a girl working in a military optical factory; or work in an aerial-torpedo factory, depicting the "life" of the torpedo from its manufacture to its final disintegration under an American hull.

Then there were the usual themes about espionage, such as *Fifth Column Fear* and *Miracle Worker*, to make the public suspicious of foreigners because "they wander about with their true intentions unknown as tourists, technicians, businessmen, students, and missionaries." The title of *The Last Days of the British Empire* is self-explanatory. A more unusual anti-British film, *International Smuggling Game*, depicted the British Consular Service running an opium smuggling ring, with which the British consul, Mr. Perkins, weaves a Machiavellian scheme for subduing Japan as the British had subdued China. *The Opium War* was also about the British stupefying the Chinese with vast quantities of the drug. *You're Being Aimed At* was about American agents trying to spread bacteriological disease throughout Japan. No doubt all this reinforced patriotic ideals and maintained the image of the Allies as nefarious villains. In this way the Japanese cinema fulfilled its wartime role.

The superiority of the Japanese over the Anglo-Saxons seemed confirmed, at least militarily, between December 1941 and June 1942. In those six months, the Japanese chased the Europeans to the limits of Eastern Asia, and overran a tenth of the surface of the globe, an area which included all French Indo-China, Thailand, Burma, the Philippines, the East Indies, and large tracts of China. To the peoples of this huge area, the "spiritual" nature of the hard Japanese rule was stressed. "This war differs from all others," wrote the Japanese-controled *Shanghai Times*, "in that it is a war of construction, not destruction. It is a 100 percent unselfish crusade undertaken by Japan in the interests of all the East Asian nations."

The new Japanese empire was disguised under the attractive name of "The Greater East Asia Co-Prosperity Sphere," in which everyone would work for the common goal of "Asia for the Asians." This latter was an excellent slogan, most fair sounding, much more precise than Hitler's "New Order." It was nothing less than the Asian version of the Monroe doctrine—just as the Co-Prosperity Sphere was the Japanese equivalent of the Allies' "Atlantic Charter." The word *kodo* was also used as the Japanese version of "the white man's burden."

That the average Japanese at home saw only idealism in the Co-Prosperity Sphere was indicated by the prize-winning titles in a competition for slogans run in early 1942 by the *Japan Times*:

1. Japanese action spells Construction
   Enemy action spells Destruction
2. With Firmness we fight
   With Kindness we build
3. Fight on until Asia is Asia's own
4. In the Freedom of the East
   Lies the Peace of the West

In an eruption of euphoria, every public meeting in Japan concluded with the singing of the *"Kimigayo,"* the national anthem, and a recital of the imperial declaration of war.

Now that the British and American imperialists had been expelled, all varieties of Asian culture, oppressed for so long, would blossom. Such phrases as "the spiritual renovation of the Philippine people" were coined. The Philippines would henceforth be able to live "in strict observance of the traditional Oriental principles." An independent Philippine government under the quisling Jorge Vargas was installed.

During the short period of fighting in the Philippines, leaflets were dropped by air to persuade the natives that the Japanese came as friends, not enemies:

Don't Obey the Americans!
Japanese forces are friends, not enemies of the Filipinos. Don't obey America's orders, which may change your city into a battlefield. Never obey them. Keep all things as they are, don't destroy anything that belongs to the Filipinos, and we shall protect you and your city.

Another said:

Save the beautiful Philippines from war's havoc! Give up at once, lay aside your arms. Don't shed your blood for America. Return, return to your own sweet homes!

To reasure the strong Catholic element in the Philippines, a leaflet was dropped which cited the support of Pope Pius XII for the Imperial Japanese Army's campaign to foster freedom of religious worship, and it promised the army's protection of the Christian churches.

During the Japanese advance through Malaya in 1942, a variety of propaganda leaflets was disseminated. One of these addressed to enemy soldiers gave instructions on how to desert: "After fixing a white cloth to your left arm, climb down to this side under cover of darkness and meet your Japanese soldier brothers. All of them are looking toward and for you."

A crude sketch on one leaflet showed British soldiers carrying off native women by force. Another showed the British carousing while the Indonesians fought. A leaflet signed by the commander of the Japanese fleet began with the biblical quotation, "Now is the time of war. Verily, this is the day of your deliverance." It assured all educated Indonesians of religious freedom and "great power."

(Below) A leaflet exhorting solidarity between Japan and the Philippines. Japanese propagandists wrote books and magazines for schoolchildren in the Co-Prosperity Sphere. For the lower grades, they produced Frontline Diary *and* The Co-Prosperity Sphere Children's Stories: *for the upper grades,* Military Talks *and* Wartime Geography. *The Japanese language was used in official documents and taught in all the schools. To reach the illiterate, Japanese propaganda was delivered by film and radio in local dialects. People in the occupied territories had to honor the emperor and celebrate Japanese festivals. For the organized reception of propaganda, Neighborhood Associations and East Asia Youth Leagues were formed.*

SHOULDER TO SHOULDER
LET US BRING UP
THE NEW PHILIPPINES

(Below and opposite page) Iva Ikuko Toguri, known to thousands of GIs in the Pacific as Tokyo Rose, was a Japanese-American with a degree in zoology from UCLA. She had visited Japan after graduation and war broke out before she could return home. She agreed to make daily broadcasts to American soldiers in the Pacific, combining popular music with a soothing patter intended to make them homesick. After the war she was convicted as a traitor, imprisoned and fined. Tokyo Rose was not the only American to broadcast to her countrymen for the enemy. The soft voice of Axis Sally, broadcasting from Berlin, was heard on European battlefronts by American troops. Like Tokyo Rose, Axis Sally was also found guilty as a traitor when the war ended.

In all these occupied countries, the Japanese immediately founded mutual cultural societies in the capital cities to ingratiate the natives, the principal aim being to foster the use of the Japanese language throughout the East, replacing English as the lingua franca. In Indonesia they also founded a more ambiguous organization, "The Virgin's Association." Its aim was "to rally all Indonesian girls to cooperate with the Japanese Army."

The vast territories which the Japanese had annexed so rapidly presented them with a number of problems similar to, but more complicated than, those which confronted the victorious Hitler in 1941. He too had bitten off more than he could immediately digest. But, as a comparison of the European and Asian maps reveals, he at least was working on interior lines, in hundreds rather than thousands of miles, and on land. The neo-Japanese empire, thousands of miles square, embraced an area which was mostly water, studded with innumerable isles of all sizes. Controling this maritime expanse politically proved to be an engineering problem, to which short-wave radio alone provided a solution.

The Japanese had had some experience with the propaganda uses of short-wave broadcasting and, lest their own people should be tainted with it from abroad, had in 1932 banned the ownership of short-wave receivers throughout Japan. Therefore the first task of the Japanese invading forces was to install a short-wave broadcasting system embracing the entire Co-Prosperity Sphere, with powerful transmitters in Batavia (Jakarta), Singapore, and Saigon. From here, night and day for the next four years, an uninterrupted flow of propaganda about Japan's plans for Asian welfare, together with denigration of the "Anglo-Saxon tyrants," poured forth.

The next immediate goal was Australasia, which was subjected throughout 1942 to this intense radio war. In attacking the "White Australian" policy which had for over a hundred years kept Australia a preserve for Europeans, the Japanese had the right approach. There were only 7 million people, nearly all of European descent, in Australia, a continent which at a conservative estimate could nourish at least 100 million. Why should the tropical northern and desert areas be kept empty, the Japanese asked, simply because no European could live in such a climate? The more industrious and frugally living Asiatics could irrigate these areas and turn them into a cornucopia. If they were prepared to come and make the Australian deserts bloom like roses, why should they be denied? Why should the Anglo-Saxons keep this vast continent entirely to themselves, in complete disregard of other people and the well-being of their neighbors?

This all went down very well in the early days when Japanese arms were everywhere triumphant. Modeling themselves on Germany, the Japanese established communal listening to this propaganda for their new subjects. Loudspeakers were hung at street corners all over the occupied territories. Known euphemistically as "singing trees" and "singing towers," they were also introduced into elementary schools throughout the

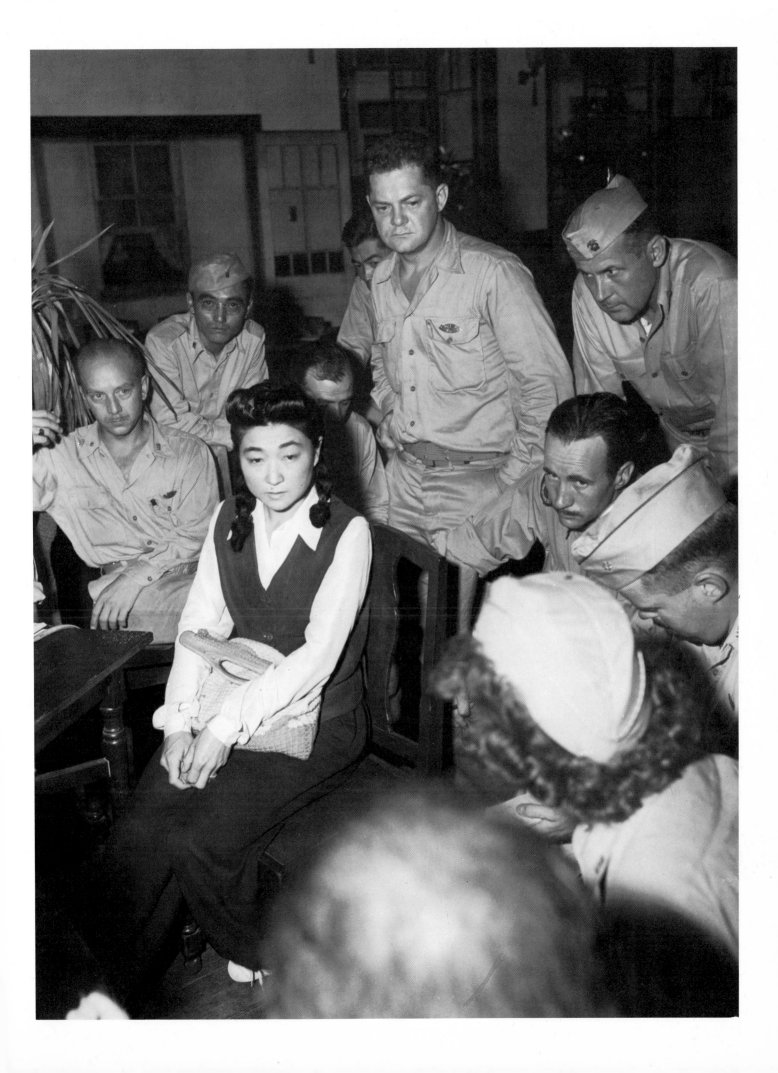

(Below) As the war progressed, the Americans dropped numerous leaflets such as this on the Japanese. The leaflets, produced by the Office of War Information, were the most effective means of propaganda in the Far East. At first they were dropped by plane on combat troops in the South Sea battle areas; but in late 1944 and until the end of the war, the home front was showered with a barrage of messages. As American bombers moved closer to Japan, the leaflet campaign was stepped up. The leaflets showed the falsehood of the Japanese government's domestic propaganda and prepared the people for surrender. In the spring and summer of 1945 leaflets fluttered down daily on Japanese cities, announcing warnings of impending bombing raids.

日本軍部首脳者に此の戦争を惹起した全責任がある

Co-Prosperity Sphere.

Particular importance was attached to India, now on the frontier of the new empire, and through which the Japanese hoped soon to pass on their way to shake hands with Hitler in Persia or Afghanistan. India was regarded as potentially part of Japan's Greater East Asian Co-Prosperity Sphere. A "Free India" radio station was installed in Saigon, which encouraged the natives of the subcontinent to rise against their aggressors while the British were weak and fully occupied elsewhere. "Indian Independence" transmitters were also set up in Bangkok and Singapore, as was an "Indian Muslim Station." The Japanese formed the "Indian National Army," with Subhas Chandra Bose as its leader. Numerous leaflets were dropped on British Indian Army troops calling on them to join the Japanese and help liberate their mother country. One gaudy leaflet showed two Indians chasing a caricature of a British soldier surrounded by his shattered equipment and tattered flag. Another anti-British leaflet declared that the Japanese army had "exterminated the diabolical British power from all parts of East Asia," and it was now time to free India for the Indians.

All this was for the benefit of the Asiatics. For the Americans, and their Australian and New Zealand allies, the leaflets and radio transmissions took another form, aimed primarily at dividing them from one another. The Americans were accused of intending to make Australia into the 49th state of the union. Pornographic leaflets were distributed to Australian troops showing Australian girls in the sexual embraces of drunken G.I.s or Tommies while their boy friends were hacking their way through the jungles of Borneo. The Australians and New Zealanders were told that the British had always made them fight Britain's battles. Their soldiers were now fighting far from home on the shores of North Africa, while the bulk of the British army was safe in its island home.

For the remaining American forces in the Pacific who had been thrown back so brusquely after Pearl Harbor, the Japanese engaged the services of a half-Japanese woman, Iva Ikuko Toguri, who had lived all her life in America, where she had obtained a degree in geology from UCLA. Affectionally known to the G.I.s as "Tokyo Rose," she used to deliver 15-minute broadcasts daily, of a sentimental nature, appealing to their natural disposition to become homesick, and describing the native land some of them would never see again. She offered excellent swing music together with husky-voiced sex talk. (After the war she was tried by the Americans and sentenced to ten years in prison and a $10,000 fine.)

Another propaganda device used on short-wave radio was the prisoner-of-war broadcast. Allied prisoners were brought before the microphone, through which they sent messages to their families at home. Statements with their names and addresses were read over the air, and the eager listeners in America and Australia were assured that their men folk were alive and well. Some of the POWs described how well they were treated, the amenities in the camps, the fresh fruit and vegetables, tobacco, sugar . . . one camp had its own bakery. The messages were ingeniously sandwiched between news items of indeterminate length, so that the relatives had to listen to the whole program in the hope of hearing the prisoner's voice.

Technically efficient as was the vast radio network, it suffered from the broadcaster's faulty pronunciation and knowledge of foreign languages. The Japanese in wartime evidently had difficulty finding good translators. Such phrases as, "With the exception of one Japanese soldier dead, all the rest were in the best of spirits," or "The remaining British planes took to their heels," or "Japanese men look furious, but they are sweet inside," made the listener smile rather than tremble. Another curious statement from Batavia in March 1943 announced that "Britain is worried by the scarcity of silk. The British government therefore contemplates taming all the silkworms of Liberia . . . . but first they must be domesticated."

A more serious Japanese shortcoming at the beginning of the war was their faulty assessment of the American character and institutions. Knowing that the American people preferred peace to war, commerce to fighting, the Japanese assumed that they were all hostile to their leaders, Roosevelt and his government, who had prepared them for war. They underestimated the effect of the Pearl Harbor attack, which they seriously believed the American people would regard as a defensive act forced on Japan by "Roosevelt and his clique." In fact, that single action at Pearl Harbor on December 7, 1941, provided the Allies with a propaganda weapon which all the skill of the Japanese propagandists could not counter—"the stab in the back." The Japanese were also unwise enough to suppose that because a large section of Congress and the Republican Party hated Roosevelt's domestic policy, they hated his foreign policy too. In other broadcasts to America they boasted that Japan's spiritual strength rendered her soldiers capable of superhuman feats, while the American high standard of living produced physical and moral weakness. This, they contended, was confirmed by the American retreats in the first six months of the Pacific war. It would be better therefore to make peace and recognize the Greater East Asia Co-Prosperity Sphere.

Another hindrance to effective propaganda was the Japanese censorship system, by which in wartime the military high command monopolized the news. The Board of Information was made subject to direct control by the army and navy. At one stage military censorship was actually imposed on news obtained from the Foreign Office from its own sources. The Domei press agency was continually being ordered by the military authorities to emit a greater flow of stories and photographs to uplift morale —a demand which was made irrespective of the war situation or the amount of news available. The army and navy did not improve matters by being at loggerheads and maintaining separate organizations for their respective propaganda. When the army announced a victory, the navy felt it must do so too. So suspicious was the army of the navy that it had its own shipyards, cargo ships, and even cargo submarines; while the navy,

(Below) In early 1945, Tokyo newspapers were claiming military victories while the Japanese defense of the Pacific was cracking. The Allied blockade had cut Japan's supplies of raw materials and the American air force had stepped up its bombing raids. General MacArthur had pushed ahead in the Philippines and the British were driving the Japanese out of Burma. Propagandists in Tokyo had promulgated the Great East Asia Co-Prosperity Sphere as a harmonious league of Asian nations led by Japan. Americans rephrased the slogan "Asia for the Asians" as "Asia for the Japanese." Late in the war, American cartoons mirrored confidence in the collapse of Japan's empire.

(Top) As the Allies piled up victories
in the Pacific, American cartoonists
indulged in a bit of muscle-flexing.
Such cartoons bolstered the public's
confidence that America would win the
Pacific war. (Bottom) Japanese home
propaganda was based on false reports
of military successes even as Japan's
hegemony in the Pacific was crumbling.

MASTERLY UNDERSTATEMENT.

not to be outdone, had its own motor corps for land transport.
The two services even maintained separate weather stations.
After Guadalcanal, they argued fiercely as to whether Australia
should be attacked directly from the sea (the navy argument),
or over land through New Guinea (the army argument). The
result was that the great Australian continent, where invasion
might have succeeded in 1942, was never attacked at all.

Nevertheless, as long as Japan was winning, these weaknesses
could be overcome. During the first six months, she had nothing
but victories to show. Although the high command exaggerated
their scope, it was telling the broad truth; Japanese propaganda
was effective both at home and abroad, in raising morale and
creating confidence in the government's ability to win the war.
After each new victory, the "singing trees" at a thousand loca-
tions throughout the Co-Prosperity Sphere blared out the
"Kaigum," the navy march.

The turning point came in May 1942, when the run of victories was halted at the battle of the Coral Sea off the north
Australian coast. Here, the advancing Japanese were surprised
to find a much revived American navy, which harried them
north, inflicting more losses than it sustained. This was followed
a month later by the more decisive battle of Midway, in which
the Americans sank four Japanese aircraft carriers—hitherto the
principal instrument of Japan's expansion. Seven months later,
when the American marines ejected the Japanese forces from
Guadalcanal in the Solomons, Japan had reached the limit of
her conquests. Thereafter, it was to be a slow but steady Japanese retreat westwards and northwards for three years, across
the great watery spaces she had so precipitately invested.

In spite of these portentous events, the Japanese high command refused to entertain even the suspicion of a defeat. The
prime minister himself, General Tojo, announced to the Diet on
May 27, 1942, that in the Coral Sea engagement, the Japanese
navy had completely annihilated the American Pacific fleet. Yet
only a month later at Midway that same fleet sank four Japanese aircraft carriers and a number of ancillary craft. The
Japanese aircraft carriers' dominion of the Pacific was over, but
their leaders refused to admit it, even to themselves. On the
obduracy of these men, a significant comment is made by Rear
Admiral Matsushima in his book The False Song of Victory,
published after the war. He reports that when news of the Midway battle was coming in, he was present in Tokyo at a naval
press-briefing conference. The sinking of four Japanese aircraft
carriers made a terrible impression. He notes the chief of the
press section saying, "The most important thing is to keep it
quiet. If ever a part of the truth becomes known, it will be difficult to control the situation." Matsushima adds, "No one spoke.
These people were not trained to defeat. Everyone sat silent
with arms folded. Thus, the naval press section fooled a nation."

If these setbacks could be concealed from the Japanese people, the daring and spectacular air raid by General Doolittle and
his B-25s on Tokyo on April 18, 1942, could not be. It gave a
galvanizing shock to the Japanese, who had been brought up for

centuries to believe that their homeland was inviolable. The newspapers naturally belittled it, presenting Doolittle and his men as "demons who carry out indiscriminate bombing attacks on innocent civilians and noncombatants." As a proof of Tokyo's excellent air-defense system, a wing and an undercarriage of a shot-down B-25 were put on show. Six months later, three of the captured Doolittle airmen were executed. This was a foolish and hypocritical act by the authors of the Pearl Harbor attack, for it stimulated violent feelings of revenge in the Americans. It was now that the image of "the Japanese ape," in film and cartoon, became popular in the United States.

After the Coral Sea and Midway battles, the Americans undertook the arduous and bloody road of "island hopping" up the reaches of the western Pacific, gradually forcing the Japanese garrisons out of the Solomons, the Martials, the Carolines, until in mid-1944 they reached the Marianas, where the great strategic prize of Saipan awaited them. On the edge of the Asiatic continental shelf, Saipan was little more than 1,500 miles from Tokyo. From there, American heavy bombers would at last have a first-class land base from which to bomb the Japanese homeland (Doolittle's raid had been carried out from aircraft carriers). After another big battle of aircraft carriers off the Marianas, the Americans successfully stormed the heavily defended island. The propaganda value of the Saipan victory was immense. Not only had the Japanese people been led to believe that Saipan was impregnable, but from here the Americans could broadcast to Japan on the medium-wave band, which the Japanese were equipped to receive. Until now, owing to the vast distances, only short-wave broadcasting of American propaganda had been possible; but it had proved of little value, because all short-wave sets had been confiscated by the police. The fall of Saipan was such a blow to Japan that it led to the resignation of General Tojo's government. As Japan now lost one strategic foothold after another in the Pacific, the militarists were forced to reverse their previous claims that these places were of great strategic importance. They now said they were valueless to the Americans. This was bad propaganda, both for home consumption and the occupied territories.

Perhaps the greatest American propaganda triumph in the Pacific war was the dropping of leaflets from the air. The first of these landed on Japanese troops during the South Seas battles of 1942. In those days the Japanese high command regarded them without undue apprehension, particularly as they suffered from an early defect of all American propaganda to Japan; they were badly translated, into a Japanese which a Japanese literary man called "as archaic as Chaucer." Their illustrations, too, were unlikely to impress the Japanese soldiery. One showed a Japanese at his meal with his chopsticks placed on either side of the plate, like the Western knife and fork; whereas the Japanese lay them parallel at the base of the plate. Some pictures showed the kimono with the left side covering the right; the Japanese wear it right over left. These are small points, but they modified any credibility in the propaganda. The same could be said of the

(Top) A cartoon by Cargill from the Flint *(Michigan)* Journal. *In early 1944, Japan still hoped to maintain control of her empire, but the massive loss of air power was a sign that it was beginning to decline. (Bottom) Propaganda for Asian villagers was crude and simple. This sign promised that the Allies would liberate Asians from the Japanese invaders.*

*(Below and opposite page) The
American bombing raid on Tokyo led
by Lieutenant Colonel James Doolittle
on April 18, 1942, came as a
psychological shock to the Japanese,
who were brought up to believe that
their homeland was impenetrable. The
newspapers pictured Doolittle's men
as demons who "carried out an
inhuman, insatiable, indiscriminate
bombing attack on the sly." As
retaliation, the captured flyers were
executed. Americans felt that the
executions had violated the rules of
warfare. President Roosevelt referred
to the "barbarous execution by the
Japanese government." Cartoons by
Edwin Marcus and Sy Moyer portrayed
the enemy as a barbarian, a familiar
propaganda device used by all
belligerents.*

early broadcast propaganda, in which the American accent of the announcer or commentator was unmistakable. Like the British at the beginning of the war, the American propagandists had a lot to learn.

As they moved closer to the Japanese archipelago, these misunderstandings of custom and language were gradually eliminated; and the leaflets, particularly those announcing the. list of places to be bombed, and which rained down in millions on the principal cities, were eagerly read by the civilian population. The Japanese were strictly forbidden to possess any of these leaflets, and were instructed, when they found them, to hand them over to the police. But when the "advance notice" of the bombing began, few people obeyed. Families read them aloud at night by concealed candlelight.

As the Americans advanced inexorably northwards, the Japanese propagandists seem to have lost their heads. They began inventing a series of nonexistent battles, as at Bougainville, in which the Americans were said to have suffered a devastating defeat. In 1942, when General MacArthur was ejecting the Japanese from Guadalcanal, they described him as "now a nervous wreck in Canberra." When in October 1943 an American task force attacked Formosa, the Japanese radio reported that seven American aircraft carriers had been sunk. In fact, two American cruisers had been damaged. As island after island was wrested from them, the militarists furnished lies, half-truths, and the suppression of truth, to such an extent that almost no announcement could be acepted at its face value. In his book *The Lost War*, the Japanese writer Masuo Kato says, "Japan was hopelessly beaten in psychological warfare, not because of any particular adroitness on the part of the Allies, but because the Allies based their propaganda on truth—whereas Japan was unwilling to deal in truth, almost from the outset."

In the last stages of the war, the Japanese propagandists fell back on "atrocity stories" in the Northcliffe manner, to whip up patriotic fervor. They said that if the Americans won, they would exterminate the entire male population of Japan and carry off all the women as paramours. All that was left for any self-respecting Japanese to do was to die for his country. After the bloody Okinawa fighting, many people in Tokyo firmly believed that every female there had been raped by at least one G. I.

A last piece of propaganda which was more effective was the public exhibition in the center of Tokyo of a B-29 bomber, which had been brought down over the city. Beside the great airplane was placed the little Japanese fighter which had shot it out of the sky. This showed how vulnerable was "America's brute force" to an individual fact of courage. The pilot of the fighter described to the press how, when he had climbed above the American giant, he had pumped his machine-gun bullets into it. He felt very small, he said, "like a peanut on a platter." Thousands flocked to admire his feat. Finally the kamikaze or suicide planes were introduced to whip up public morale and induce a spirit of imitation. Loaded with bombs and torpedoes,

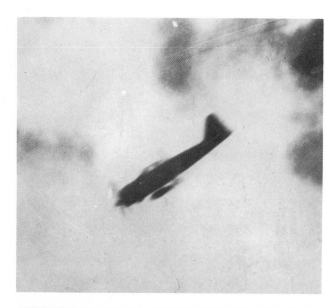

(Top) A Japanese suicide plane starts its dive toward a U.S. warship in the Western Pacific. Kamikaze pilots were told that the salvation of Japan depended on them and that it was an honor to die for the Emperor. (Bottom) A painting which idealized the young Japanese air cadets who were ready to rush forth and defend the homeland.

their pilots would deliberately crash them and themselves into the deck or sides of American vessels.

Similar sacrifices, if not as extreme, were demanded from the whole people; and for a time they gave of their best. Even when it was clear to them that Japan was losing, most Japanese had become so indoctrinated with the concept of *kokutai* that they clung to the belief that "God's country" could not possibly lose a war. Japan *must* be invincible, and they were told that "the decisive battle which is to destroy America is yet to be fought." But at this moment the Japanese navy, which alone could fight that battle, had virtually ceased to exist. In desperation, the leaders persuaded the people that voluntary self-deprivation was a hidden resevoir of strength. To go without food—and the supply situation was becoming hopeless—was to demonstrate one's powers of resistance. Radio Tokyo told citizens that "the strength is raised by the victory of the spirit." In the air-raid shelters as the bombs rained down they were told, and they believed, that calisthenics could make hungry men vigorous again.

Some people may see great virtue in the Japanese stoicism, as the defeats piled up and ship after ship, aircraft carrier after aircraft carrier, the only lines of defense, sank. People may well admire the Japanese concern over how to appear dignified in the eyes of the world, how not to lose face, when things are going badly. Right up to the end, Japanese sailors were instructed that if they had to abandon ship, they must man the lifeboats with the utmost decorum, or they would become the laughing stock of the world. "The Americans," they were told, "will make movies of you, and show them in New York."

By the beginning of 1945, everyone realized that the loss of territory was more serious than the official communiqués admitted. Toward the end, Domei took the daring and unprecedented step of carrying out an opinion poll. A fair proportion of the voters, while still intensely patriotic, expressed dissatisfaction with the misinformation or lack of information from official sources; they asked that more facts about the war be made public.

The approaching end became clear with the Potsdam Declaration of 1945. This was withheld from the Japanese people by their rulers; but they were told about it in the leaflets dropped in millions by American airplanes all over the home islands. From the Allied demand for unconditional surrender to be followed immediately by military occupation of their islands, they learned the extent of the disaster. The disillusion with their leaders was complete.

Then came the two atom bombs, followed by the final and most decisive propaganda campaign of the war, which saved perhaps hundreds of thousands of lives. In July 1945 the Japanese government had informed Washington through the neutrals that it was prepared to discuss peace terms. This would involve bargaining; and in order to secure a good position, the Japanese leaders decided not to inform their people of the negotiations. The Office of War Information therefore informed them in its own way. At dawn on August 14, 1945, American aircraft dropped some 3 million leaflets on Tokyo and the principal Japanese cities, announcing that the Japanese government had asked for talks. This effectively countered the objections by the powerful die-hard element in the Japanese cabinet who wanted to refuse the American terms and go on fighting. Peace would have come finally, it is true, but only after much more bloodshed. After the war, Japanese officials admitted that once their people knew that peace was being discussed, the government had no alternative but to accept the American terms. As an American State Department official later put it, "This one leaflet operation alone probably repaid the entire cost of OWI throughout the whole war."

Few propagandists can have had such difficult problems to face as had the Japanese in World War II. They were hamstrung and frequently misled by conflicting directives from the prime minister's office, the army headquarters, the navy headquarters. They were restricted on all sides by stringent censorship regulations, by red tape and official refusal to face facts. Had they been allowed, they might have turned the slogan "Asia for the Asians" to good account; for the Japanese success in the early days of the war in the occupied countries was due almost exclusively to this Asian racial appeal, the call to rid the Pacific of the European whites who had no business there, and to develop the great empty spaces of Australia, for example, with the native peoples of Oceania. They had a trump card in their hands, but they proved incapable of playing it. Any advantage that accrued from it was abrogated by the harsh nature of their rule. Unaccustomed to dominion over other nations, as rulers they proved inflexible and illiberal. When they made concessions to their new subjects, these were patently tactical, to be withdrawn when the war was won. Thus, they granted independence to Burma, on the periphery of their new empire and therefore harder to control, or to the Filipinos, who were the most advanced and numerous, but withheld it from Indonesia (although originally promised), and from Malaya, both of which their navy could dominate.

Another reason for their failure as colonizers was their inability to replace the flow of material goods provided by the Anglo-Americans during the latter's suzerainty. This was especially evident in the Philippines, whose upper classes were accustomed to American automobiles, refrigerators, and all those other mechanical devices which are regarded throughout the world as the symbols of civilization. When the Japanese failed to provide these, the natives soon lost confidence in all the Japanese talk of the Co-Prosperity Sphere.

The Allies were quick to realize this, and in their propaganda to the occupied territories they told the natives they were now living in a "Co-Poverty Sphere." Their constant theme was that all the Asian aspirations to independence were being thwarted as the Japanese destroyed the existing well-balanced economy, and turned the area into "Asia for the Japanese." So Japan fell as her allies had, one three months before, the other two years before. The famous Berlin-Rome-Tokyo axis had lasted a little

(Top) Propaganda leaflets such as this one were dropped on Japan at the rate of one million daily. The message stressed peace with honor, even under terms of unconditional surrender. The leaflet included quotes from President Truman's VE-day speech on surrender. (Bottom) A leaflet interpreting Roosevelt's "Four Freedoms" to the Japanese.

(Top) The second atomic bomb was dropped on Nagasaki in August 1945. The devastating blast prompted Japan's surrender but cost tens of thousands of lives. (Bottom) A panoramic view of Hiroshima after the atomic explosion. Within moments the entire city was razed. The destruction caused by the atomic bombs was unprecented in the history of mankind.

over five years. There were similarities between the Axis powers, between East and West, such as the insistence on military indoctrination, and the Japanese belief, as in Germany, that she was a country with a destiny; and that war pays. But fascism or Nazism in the European sense did not develop in Japan. There were no party organizations which virtually ran the country and tightly controled the propaganda media. No demagogue of the Hitler-Mussolini variety emerged; there was no undue concentration of power in the hands of one individual. The Japanese military leaders shared responsibility, argued fiercely with one another, and governed by compromise among themselves. They never promised their people a short war, as the Nazis did. On the contrary, they always said it was impossible to foresee its end. Their early victories were interpreted not as having an immediate, decisive effect but rather a future, cumulative one, in a struggle which could last a hundred years. It lasted exactly three years and four months.

Issued to commemorate the Conscription Law, effective
June 1, 1941 / Manchukuo / Artist unknown.

Co-Prosperity Sphere solidarity, c. 1943/
Japanese magazine cover/Artist unknown.

(Top) Issued in commemoration of the 2600th anniversary
of the birth of the Japanese Empire, 1940/Manchukuo/
Artist unknown. (Bottom) Issued for the 10th anniversary
of the creation of Manchukuo, 1942/Japan/Artist unknown.

Japan proclaims her role as Asia's leader,
c. 1943/Japanese leaflet/Artist unknown.

Propaganda against the Allies, c. 1943/
Japan/M. Tsurui Hodoobu.

PAHLAWAN-TANK
NISHIZOEMI

"The Story of Tank Commander Nishizumi," c. 1942/ Japanese film poster for occupied Indonesia/Artist unknown.

"National Savings Bond Drive," no date/Japan/ Artist unknown.

"Towards a Scientific Japan. Exhibition of Inventions," no date/Japan/Artist unknown.

"Zip up your lips," no date/Japan/ Artist unknown.

Japanese sex leaflets were amusing but ineffectual, no date/Japan/Artist unknown.

*Australians fighting on New Guinea received
such leaflets, no date/Japan/Artist unknown.*

*Aussie women at home were said to be unfaithful,
no date/Japanese leaflet/Artist unknown.*

The Japanese harped unsuccessfully on the infidelity
theme, no date / Japanese leaflet / Artist unknown.

Commemorative issues, 1939–1945/
China/Artist unknown.

Published by United China Relief, c. 1943/
USA/Martha Sawyers.

中美偉大領袖
爲公理
自由
奮鬥！
美國政府宣傳部印發

Poster affirming U.S. support for Chiang Kai-shek,
c. 1942/USA for China/Wong Siuling.

WINSTON S. CHURCHILL

FRANKLIN D. ROOSEVELT

JOSEPH STALIN

CHIANG KAI-SHEK

Chiang joins the Big Three in this poster, no date/England/Artist unknown.

An American aviator portrayed as a war god,
no date/USA poster for China/Artist unknown.

"The Indies must be free," 1945/Holland/
Nico Broekman.

New Zealand was a U.S. ally in the Pacific, no date/USA/Duco.

Poster to strengthen resistance in the Philippines c. 1943/USA/Artist unknown.

ASKARI WETU WASHINDA WAJAPANI

Smash the Japs!

African soldiers were recruited to fight Japan,
no date/England/Roland Davies.

INDIE MOET VRIJ !

WERKT EN VECHT ERVOOR !

"Work and fight to free the Indies," 1944/British
poster for the Dutch government/Pat Keely.

U.S. leaflets warned the Japanese of renewed might
after Germany's surrender, 1945/USA/Artist unknown.

ATTENTION AMERICAN SOLDIERS!

I CEASE RESISTANCE

THIS LEAFLET GUARANTEES HUMANE TREATMENT TO ANY JAPANESE DE-SIRING TO CEASE RESISTANCE. TAKE HIM IMMEDIATELY TO YOUR NEAREST COMMISSIONED OFFICER.

By Direction of the Commander in Chief.

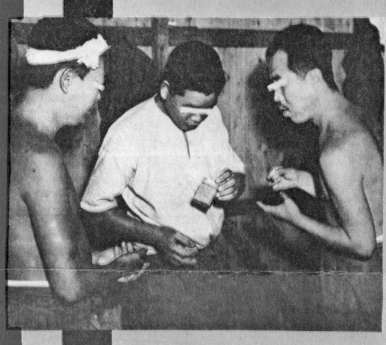

（日本の家族保護の為の目隠し）

上の英文の内容は「この人は最早敵でな
く國際條約により生命、衣食住は勿論
醫療等が完全に保証さるべき者なりと
云ふ意味が書かれて居る
左圖は既に當方に来て居られる諸君の
戰友の一部

17-J-1

Leaflets guaranteed humane treatment to Japanese who surrendered, c. 1945/USA/Artist unknown.

Afterword
By Daniel Lerner

The Psychological Warfare Campaign Against Germany:
D-Day to V-E Day

America entered World War II with a big bang at Pearl Harbor. It ended World War II with the even bigger bangs at Hiroshima and Nagasaki. Between these explosions a great deal of warfare occurred that was labeled "psychological." Psychological warfare is as old as Joshua's trumpets at the walls of Jericho and the rumors whispered about Hannibal. In World War II, however, psychological warfare became a major part of overall military strategy and an integral part of the military structure. The integration of the Psychological Warfare Division (PWD) into General Eisenhower's staff created a new dimension in the history of persuasive communication linked to cohesive action.

The historic role of wartime propaganda is exemplified by the "siege of the city."[1] Its purpose was to reduce military strongpoints and supply centers. A great variety of ingenious techniques were evolved through the centuries. We cannot vouch for the effectiveness of Joshua's trumpets, which he sounded seven times as he circled Jericho "and the walls came tumbling down." Nor is any hard data available on the utility of the Hittite ritual of *evocatio,* prayers designed to induce the protective gods of the besieged city to "transmigrate" into one's own camp and leave the enemy defenseless. We do know, however, that the Trojan Horse devised by the Greeks enabled them to infiltrate and undermine the mighty fortress-city of antiquity.

The siege of the city still plays a wartime role, albeit one greatly transformed by the development of long-range artillery in World War I ("Big Bertha") and strategic aircraft in World War II ("Flying Fortress"). Pablo Picasso's *Guernica* and Archibald MacLeish's radio play "Fall of the City" vividly dramatize the newer techniques used in the Spanish prelude to World War II. During that war the "strategic" bombing of enemy cities became a conventional procedure of air warfare. When the Germans used their pilotless V-1 and V-2 against Britain they called the tactic *Wunderwaffen* (wonder weapons); when the Allied air forces used it against German cities they called it *Terrorangriff* (terror attack).[2]

So, while classic psychological warfare played a role

in the siege of such German cities as Willingen and Aachen, the main action was preempted by the new military technology. As a result, the basic military conception of the urban center was transformed. The fortress-city has virtually disappeared from the world, since it cannot possibly be defended against artillery and aircraft. The military importance of the city today is as an industrial center, as the producer of materiel for the fighting forces. World War II propaganda was transformed accordingly. In the phrase then current, it was aimed at "the man behind the man behind the gun."[3] This concept has been carried even further under the Cold War policy of "mutual deterrence." Both the U.S. and the U.S.S.R. have deployed their nuclear missiles so as to destroy each other's key industrial cities if war occurs. It is this threat of reciprocal destruction that has maintained the unnerving "balance of terror" over the past two decades.[4]

This glimpse of the historical terrain indicates that propaganda always has been, and remains today, an instrument of policy. Propagandists do not make policy; they devise strategies of symbol manipulation to implement policies made by others. Indeed, propaganda is but one of the four main instruments used by policymakers. The other three are diplomacy, economics, and military action, all of which affect the material environment in which people live. Propaganda is the distinctive instrument which manipulates only the symbols by which people think, feel, believe; it works with threats and promises to affect people's hopes and fears. It shapes human aspirations to what should happen and human expectations of what will happen.

As money is to an economy, so symbols are to all communication—the medium of exchange, the measure of value, the tie that binds past and present to the future. When communication seeks to persuade—i.e., when it operates as propaganda—it manipulates symbols to shape attitudes that will condition (facilitate or constrain) the

---

[1] For fuller discussion see my book *Psychological Warfare against Nazi Germany* (The M.I.T. Press, paperback, 1971) pp. 272–281.

[2] For a detailed report and evaluation see U.S. Strategic Bombing Survey, *Effects of Strategic Bombing on German Morale* (Washington, 1947).

[3] A critical analysis of this concept is made by Hans Speier, "Psychological Warfare Reconsidered" in Daniel Lerner, ed., *Propaganda in War and Crisis* (Arno Press, 1972) pp. 463–492.

[4] An early diagnosis of "atomic blackmail" was made by Hans Speier in *Social Order and The Risks of War* (The M.I.T. Press, 1967). Two much-discussed French interpretations are Pierre Gallois, *The Balance of Terror* (Houghton Mifflin, 1961) and Daniel Lerner & Raymond Aron, eds. *France Defeats E.D.C.* (Praeger, 1957). An important (though highly unofficial) current perspective is that of the eminent Soviet physicist published by *The New York Times* as "The Sakharov Manuscript."

future behavior of its "targets." In the wartime context, propaganda targets are differentiated into four main classes: enemies, allies, neutrals, and the home front. To each of these targets, propagandists adapt their strategies and vary their tactics. To the enemies, propaganda strategy centers around the theme of their ultimate defeat; to the allies, the stress is on loyalty, unity, ultimate triumph; to the neutrals, propagandists stress their righteousness and inevitable triumph; the home front is constantly reminded of the need for effort and sacrifice to achieve victory.

Underlying all variations of strategy and tactic, however, is a single propaganda *process* which always involves the same components: a sender, a message, a receiver, a purpose, a technique, and an effect. These are the six main variables in the propaganda process, identified nearly a half-century ago by Harold D. Lasswell, which formed the celebrated paradigm: Who says what to whom, why, how, with what effects?[5]

Let us focus our attention upon Nazi Germany as the enemy target of psychological warfare in the ETO (European Theater of Operations), in particular upon the campaign waged, from D-Day to V-E Day, by PWD/SHAEF (Psychological Warfare Division/Supreme Headquarters Allied Expeditionary Force) under General Eisenhower. In setting the context for psychological warfare against Nazi Germany, it is essential to recall that the allied, neutral, and home front audiences were a pervasive presence in the deliberations of top Allied policymakers. World War II was fought by a gigantic coalition of independent nations and governments-in-exile (mainly in London). Coalitions are, by their nature, a temporary form of association based on the agreement to submerge differences over what one is *for* in order to combat what all are *against*. This situation was faced squarely by Winston Churchill when he told a House of Commons hotly debating war aims with some opposition to unconditional surrender as supreme policy:

I see that in some quarters I am expected today to lay out, quite plainly and decisively, the future plan of world organization, and also to set the Atlantic Charter in its exact and true relation to subsequent declarations and current events. It is easier to ask such questions than to answer them. We are working with thirty-three United Nations and, in particular, with two great Allies who, in some forms of power, far excel the British Empire. It would be a great mistake for me, as head of the British Government, or, I may add, for this House, to take it upon ourselves to lay down the law to all those different countries, including the two great Powers with which we have to work, if the world is to be brought back into a good condition.[6]

This, then, sets the context in which psychological warfare against Nazi Germany had to be conducted. It is hard to imagine a global coalition led by four more diverse major partners than the U.S., U.S.S.R., Great Britain, and Kuomintang (Chiang Kai-shek's) China. Add to these several dozen other nations defeated and occupied by the Nazis, often represented in Allied councils by governments-in-exile with disparate voices and divergent priorities. If one recalls the problems presented to Allied policymakers by only one such exile, General de Gaulle as self-designated leader of the Free French, one can hear the bewildering cacophony that resonates through Churchill's tempered tones in his speech to Parliament.

Given such a coalition engaged in a total war that was also a global war, it is difficult to conceive any supreme policy other than the unconditional surrender of the Axis powers on which the Allied spokesmen could have agreed. While the policy applied as well to Fascist Italy and Imperial Japan, it was clearly the Nazi hegemony over Europe that had to be completely broken to achieve the Allies' central purpose. It was to this purpose that the propaganda campaign executed by PWD/SHAEF addressed itself.

In considering the organization of PWD for this purpose, it is essential to note that PWD was a "special staff section" under the command of General Eisenhower's Supreme Headquarters. PWD received much help from such civilian agencies as the OWI (Office of War Information) and the OSS (Office of Strategic Services) in the U.S., and and from civilian agencies such as the BBC (British Broadcasting Corporation) and the PWE (Political Warfare Executive) in Great Britain. Key personnel

---

[5] Harold D. Lasswell, *Propaganda Technique in World War I* (The M.I.T. Press, 1971).

[6] British Information Service, *A Selection From Speeches Made By Winston Churchill. . . .* (New York, 1943) unpaged.

had been "seconded" to PWD from these civilian agencies.

Most of them, whether they had official or "assimilated" military ranks, were civilians at heart with impressive experience and skills in symbol manipulation. Colonel William S. Paley, president of the Columbia Broadcasting System (CBS), was flanked by a trio of top people from the National Broadcasting Corporation (NBC). The late C. D. Jackson, senior executive of Time-Life, rode herd on an able battalion of researchers, writers, and editors. Colonel (now Judge) Murray I. Gurfein headed an intelligence section staffed mainly by American and British social scientists. PWD's most brilliant propaganda strategist, Richard H. S. Crossman, was a don at Oxford who became a postwar Labour M.P., member of the cabinet, editor of *The New Statesman,* and columnist for *The Daily Mirror.* Saul K. Padover, PWD's senior field analyst, recently retired as dean of The New School and Graduate Faculty in New York, where he continues to serve as professor of history and politics—as does Michael Balfour, deputy chief of intelligence, in Britain. Martin F. Herz, PWD's chief leaflet writer, has become a United States ambassador.

Given such a roster of civilian intellectuals as its cadre, it was natural that PWD experienced a quantity of problems with military discipline. One colleague, now an eminent professor of sociology at Chicago, got his head bashed in by a German bomb because he was working late at the office instead of being asleep in his barracks. This writer was court-martialed because he was working late at night in his quarters instead of minding the phone as duty officer in the general's office. (Both were awarded Purple Hearts and Bronze Stars before World War II ended in the ETO.)

While such "Little Willie" stories may convey a sense of amusement at intellectuals-in-uniform, it is important that PWD was a military formation in fact. It was commanded by General Robert A. McClure, who reported through the military chain of command to General Eisenhower himself. It was, despite its frequent aberrations, subject to military discipline and military decision. The importance of this, for propaganda strategy, is illustrated by a confrontation between Winston Churchill and General Eisenhower.

Churchill took a keen and continuous interest in what he called "the propaganda side." On one occasion he stormed into SHAEF headquarters, waving one of our leaflets, with the command: "Kill this!"[7] Churchill objected that we didn't need to "plead" with dockworkers to keep their docks in working order for our purpose in Germany; we had enough docks already, and we could open others as we needed them. Had we heeded Churchill, our psychological warfare campaign would have lost the power latent in this relatively minor manifest message. For while Churchill was right on the reality of the North Sea ports, he was quite wrong on the psychology of this leaflet. Its latent message went far beyond the issue of dockage to tell readers such things as: we are winning and our final victory will come soon; you can do nothing to change this but may make life easier for you and yours, after our victory, by doing as we tell you; thus your own future, under our dispensation, depends on what you do now.

This leaflet, and dozens like it addressed to towns and cities *before* strategic bombing, was primarily designed to reduce resistance and habituate German civilians to obeying Allied instructions. It was on this ground that PWD defended the leaflet series against Churchill's airy dismissal and won its case at the highest decision-making level of SHAEF. Whatever the future need for dockage might be, there was a clear and present Allied interest in persuading German civilians to cease resistance and obey our orders.

Such a propaganda strategy was required by the supreme policy of unconditional surrender. If the Germans were to surrender with no conditions of their own making, if their postwar lives were to be shaped by Allied decisions and directives, then it was essential to put them through a training course in obedience. In the final phase of the war (after the failure of the von Rundstedt offensive at Christmas 1944) obedience training became a major objective of PWD propaganda. With German soldiers in retreat, German civilians in disarray, and German authority in doubt, PWD output in all media began to issue instructions and orders under the joint Allied authority represented by SHAEF.

---

[7] The full text of this leaflet, W.G. 54, "To the Workers and Port Officials of Hamburg!", is reproduced in Lerner, *Psychological Warfare against Nazi Germany,* p. 238.

We have illustrated above the issuance of such instructions to dockworkers in all the principal port cities of Germany. Similar leaflets and broadcasts were directed to factory workers in major war-production industries (sometimes in the form of little "sabotage kits" with precise instructions on how to use them supplied by the "black operators" at PWD and elsewhere). Detailed instructions on the use of bomb shelters, storm cellars, outlying forests were directed to residents of cities targeted for imminent strategic bombing. All these efforts, which Churchill erroneously interpreted as "being kind" to the Germans, in fact laid the groundwork for their passive acquiescence and even active cooperation with the Allied military government that was soon to be running all of Germany.

Obedience training for the German soldiers was even more subtle and, especially among those who felt defeated and demoralized, more effective. The classic example was the *Passierschein* (safe conduct pass) leaflet. Its intention was clearly to provide German soldiers willing to surrender with an authority for doing so. Everything about the leaflet was designed to appear *authoritative*: the format, handsomely engraved on good paper in a rich color, has been described as "looking like a college diploma;" the language of the text was formal and official; the art work consisted mainly of the British and American army seals and the signature of General Eisenhower as Supreme Commander.

To carry out such a campaign—a campaign designed to prepare German soldiers, civilians, officials for what was actually going to happen to them during the military operations and after their unconditional surrender—required nothing less than what PWD called a "strategy of truth." Since PWD was not a troop of boy scouts, but a military formation directed to win a total war at the lowest possible cost, this requires some exegesis. A strategy of truth, it should be noted at the outset, is not synonymous with honesty. Conversely, there is no known national propaganda apparatus which operates according to a strategy of dishonesty. The word to be emphasized, in the first instance, is not "truth" but "strategy," for truth in propaganda is a function of effectiveness. The basis of operations described by the phrase is expediency, even if its rationalization to the public is usually made in terms of morality. Propagandists do not decide to tell the truth because they personally are honest, any more than they decide to tell lies because they are dishonest. Given a particular audience to be reached with a particular policy, the basis for decision is an estimate of what will work.

Such an estimate may be conditioned by the characteristics of the propagandist. Wallace Carroll, for example, describes the inclination of OWI propagandists toward a strategy of truth in these terms:

> Many of us in OWI were strongly predisposed by our previous training in favor of a program of information. Take Elmer Davis, for example. . . . Edward Klauber, Ed Barrett, Ferdinand Kuhn, and I had also been trained in the traditions of American journalism. Our inclination, too, was to put the facts of the war before the world. These facts were so overwhelmingly in favor of the Allies and they would therefore—presumably—work for an Allied victory.

These men inclined toward a strategy of truth less because they were virtuous (though they were surely that) than because of their previous training as journalists. In any case, as propagandists they defended their inclinations in the pragmatic terms that such a strategy would "presumably work for an Allied victory." When their inclinations could not be justified in these terms—i.e., when the presentation of straight facts presumably would *not* help an Allied victory—the decision went the other way. On this point, Mr. Carroll testifies obliquely:

> Our real difficulties came over a choice between giving the news and withholding it, between the practices of journalism and the dictates of war, between the urge to inform and the passion to save lives, between common honesty and plain humanity.

The policymakers at PWD were also coy, but somewhat more explicit, about distinguishing the strategy of truth from the concept expressed by the phrase "the truth, the whole truth, and nothing but the truth." In fact, there was general recognition that some truths were to be modified and other truths were to be omitted altogether. The *Standing Directive for Psychological Warfare*, which was the basic statement of policy for all PWD personnel, made the following discreet provision:

> It is recognized that in the execution of Psychological Warfare it is a fundamental principle not to antagonize

the audience. Direct denunciation or direct offence against known susceptibilities will therefore be avoided in all Psychological Warfare against the enemy armed forces.

This eliminated undue preoccupation of propagandists with "the whole" truth. The *Standing Directive* also made clear that PWD was not confined to "nothing but" the truth, by restricting its instructions to overt propaganda. Overt, or "white," propaganda was the only form of PWD output which identified itself to the German audience as an Allied source. The rule of accurate reporting, or at least its negative version, which prohibited deviation from the truth in statements that could be verified by the German audience, had to be strictly observed in white psychological warfare. No such restriction was placed upon the covert "gray" and "black" forms of PWD output. Gray propaganda, which omitted all mention of source, specialized precisely in *not* telling "the whole" truth. Black propaganda, which identified itself by a false source, may be viewed as, in the last analysis, a specialty in telling "anything but" the truth.

The theory was that by leading this double life, PWD could carry on like a wanton woman in the covert forms, while protecting the good name of SHAEF in white output. Since white was the only form that accurately identified itself, it was felt that nothing could be "pinned on" the Allies officially as a result of covert lying. The extent to which the Allies have been officially protected by this stratagem is questionable, in view of the postwar disclosures about covert operations which former propagandists have been permitted to publish. The actual, which is perhaps more important than official, protection of the Allied reputation for honesty by this stratagem is even more questionable. We do not know how many Germans were actually deceived as to the source of covert Allied propaganda—though what intelligence reports we received indicate that many were not deceived. Clearly the two chief gray media—the newspaper *Nachrichten für die Truppe* (*News for the Troops*) and the radio station *Soldatensender West*—were pretty generally identified with Allied sources by members of their German audience.

Most interesting and relevant to the present discussion was the agreement among propaganda experts in the covert forms that, for the most part, and particularly in the early stages of any covert campaign, they too were obliged to observe the rule of accurate reporting. The simple reason was that, in order ultimately to persuade their audience, they first had to make the audience believe them. This is one of the few dogmas advanced by PWD policymakers that seems likely to endure as an axiom of propaganda: Credibility is a condition of persuasion. Before you can make a man do what you say, you must make him believe what you say. A necessary condition for gaining his credence is that you do not permit him to catch you in lies. Hence the constraint upon all propagandists to accurate reporting of matters which are subject to verification by the audience. As the official historian put it:

Such truth [in propaganda], to be sure, can, and sometimes must, be selective, for often the truth is not credible to the enemy. However, selective or not, use by overt propaganda of falsehoods *which can be proved false by the enemy* is the same as killing the goose that might eventually lay golden eggs. (italics mine)

This constraint operates upon all propagandists, irrespective of the country or policy they serve. The Nazi propagandists had to observe the rule of accurate reporting, when they wanted to be believed, just as carefully as the Allies. Mr. Crossman writes:

It is not my impression that German propaganda was guilty of many deliberate lies. . . . Most of the German lies . . . were probably sheer mistakes, just as most of the German promises . . . were due to the ineptness of politicians. Goering was not knavish but foolish when he once stated in a speech that not a bomb would fall on the Ruhr, and so was Hitler, in October 1941, when he announced the final collapse of the Bolshevists. . . . There is every likelihood that Goebbels, the arch propagandist, was furious when such statements were made. He was far too able a man to make silly propaganda "commitments" or to perpetrate small lies deliberately. He understood that, if you want to put over a big lie, the way to do it is to be as scrupulously accurate as possible about small facts.

This brings us to the nub of the problem of truth. If all propagandists are equally committed to accurate reporting of verifiable facts, how is the Allied strategy of truth to be distinguished from the Nazi strategy of the big lie?

A general answer might be framed thus: The Allies attempted to convey a true impression of their basic policy intentions; the Nazis attempted to convey a false impression of their basic policy intentions.

The Nazis, in brief, *believed* that the Germans were a master race, and *intended* that they should establish their rule over Europe and beyond. They *said*, however, that they believed in a European culture (particularly French culture when addressing the French, particularly Italian culture when addressing the Italians, whom they off-the-record referred to as *"dreckige italienische Schweine,"* and so forth) and intended to establish a "new order" in which all Europeans could share equitably. They intended to *rule* Europe, but they pretended that they wanted only to *save* Europe from the Bolshevik menace. Thus their accuracy on details must be located within a context of overall falsehood.

The Allies, on the other hand, *believed* that Nazism was a menace to Western civilization and world peace, and *intended* to destroy it completely. They *said* the same thing in all their propaganda, no matter to whom addressed. Allied inaccuracies, and even chicaneries, on details can thus be located within a context of overall truth.

The Nazis relied on accurate reporting of details to build credibility for a propaganda campaign which was a great sham—a systematic misrepresentation of their overall policy. This is the procedure of black psychological warfare and, when elevated to the guidance of national propaganda, it becomes a strategy of the big lie. Conversely, since Allied propaganda faithfully reflected the policy intentions of its political leadership, it can appropriately be designated, despite frequent inaccuracies and occasional untruths, as a strategy of truth.

Allied strategy was the outcome of the decision, once unconditional surrender was settled as basic policy, to acknowledge and publicize it rather than to conceal it. In making *this* decision, Allied policymakers showed a greater regard for ethical considerations than did their Nazi counterparts, and perhaps a greater political wisdom than did those propagandists who tried to seduce them into modifying the policy for propaganda purposes. It was Roosevelt and Churchill, in refusing to permit PWD propagandists to falsify their actual intention with

"softening" promises to the Germans, who were responsible for the Allied strategy of truth. Just as it was Hitler, in allowing his actual policies to be modified and falsified by the propagandists, who was responsible for the Nazi strategy of the big lie.

A strategy of truth for the Nazis would have entailed a consistent campaign to persuade Europe to accept a hegemony organized under the superior German "race." Thus Nazi propaganda would have reflected faithfully Nazi intentions (i.e., policy decisions), even though it might not have succeeded any better than the attempt to deceive Europe into believing that Nazi hegemony was identical with European comity. It was not Nazi lying alone that lost them the war, any more than truthfulness alone would have won it. Had their power been sufficient, they might have accomplished their purpose despite the big lie. Dictatorship, accepting the view that dissent which can not be eliminated by persuasion can always be eliminated by coercion, need not emphasize peaceful cooperation among its long-term goals.

For the democratic process, however, which bases itself on the freely given consent of the governed, coercion must be held to a minimum, and persuasion is the key to government. On any long-term basis, credibility is a condition of persuasiveness and credence is associated with a reputation for truthfulness. Democracy, by its nature, is a long-run operation, and its distinctive function as government by consent must be affiliated with a strategy of truth. The matter is aptly summarized in a remark attributed to Abraham Lincoln, that one cannot fool all of the people all of the time. This is a view basic to democratic procedures. If the success of your government depends on fooling people (i.e., the big lie), then you must be prepared to chop off the heads of people who are not fooled. If you do not intend to govern by execution, but by consent, then you can not rely upon fooling people.

It would be misleading, as we have seen, to score the Allies 100 percent for truth and the Nazis 100 percent for falsehood. Policymaking in practice is a continuous compromise of ethics by power, of what is desirable by what is possible, and the decisive aspect of the compromise is the tendency it emphasizes. It was a matter of emphasis, in this crucial sense, that distinguished the Allied strategy of truth from the Nazi strategy of the big lie. The PWD campaigns conducted on both sides of the battlefront had the same general objectives:

(1) to help win the war by facilitating enemy surrender

(2) to help secure desirable conditions of peace (war aims)

We have seen that the Nazi emphasis on the first objective derived from the view that, once the war was won, desirable conditions of peace could be imposed by force and fiat. The Allied leadership, however, recognized that they would be in no position, at war's end, to impose conditions on all the world by force and fiat. They were confronted by a varied coalition whose wishes concerning the conditions of peace would have to be accommodated within a framework of discussion and consent. In such a situation, their emphasis had to be upon the second objective, that of maximizing the prospects for a desirable peace, without unduly compromising the first. The *Standing Directive* is very clear and firm on this cardinal point:

> The use of Psychological Warfare in military operations must be strictly subordinated to the long-term policy of our Governments, in the sense that nothing must be done with the object of undermining fighting morale during operations which would prejudice Government policy to Germany after the war. (Section 7)

The basic Allied policy being unconditional surrender, the strategy of truth required that no PWD activity should convey the impression to any German audience that other, more acceptable, terms might be arranged. Here, again, the *Standing Directive* was forceful and explicit:

> It has also been made clear by our Governments that they are determined to destroy not only the Nazi system, but the concept of the Wehrmacht, which has been both the initiator and the willing instrument of recurring German attempts to dominate other peoples. Nothing in the implementation of this directive must compromise that issue. (Section 3)

Thus the policy of unconditional surrender, interpreted according to the strategy of truth, defined the limits within which PWD was to operate. The propaganda tactics which PWD developed within these limits to guide its operation merit examination here.

The basic tactics were set down clearly in the *Standing*

Directive:

> No specific promises will be made concerning the treatment of Germany after the war, other than those expressly made by Government spokesmen. In particular there must be no suggestion that the Atlantic Charter applies to Germany by right.

Lest this general guidance be read ambiguously, the *Standing Directive* then went on to list seven specific points that had to be emphasized—and could not, in any case, be violated—by the tacticians of PWD psychological warfare:

(1) Demilitarization of Germany

(2) Punishment of war criminals

(3) Liberation of territories overrun by Nazi Germany, including Austria

(4) Occupation of Germany

(5) Destruction of Nazism and German militarism

(6) Prevention of such economic distress in Germany as will be detrimental to the rest of the world

(7) Ultimate restoration of Germany to a place "in the world family of democratic nations"

The basic techniques by which these tactics were carried out came to be grouped together as strange bedfellows called "factualism and indirection." Factualism required PWD propagandists, at the least, to avoid telling lies that could readily be detected by the targeted audience. In any case, after the successful landings at D-Day and the rapid race across France by General Patton's Third Army in the summer of 1944, it was clear that the facts of Allied military superiority, when skillfully arranged and presented, could speak for themselves. The techniques of indirection were recommended in every case. The *Directive* advised: "Treat the German as a man who, if openly incited by the enemy to cowardice, will do the opposite." Or again, in discussing the PWD line on strategic bombing:

> "Fear propaganda" designed to intensify the effect of bombs has been rendered unnecessary by the bombs themselves. . . . Avoid giving any impression that we are trying to break German morale. Seek *indirectly* to arouse resentment against the fact that air power, which the Nazis claimed as their invention, has now been turned against Germany.

The basis for factualism, which was an application of

the strategy of truth to the writing of propaganda texts, has already been discussed. The basis for indirection was an estimate of the responses which the human organism makes to verbal symbols offered by an enemy in time of war. In general, even cursory examination of the record, or reflection on the logic of the situation, supports the view that the enemy's symbols are naturally suspect. Those themes or symbols which obviously serve the enemy's interests are worse than useless: they not only fail to secure the desired effect, but often encourage the reverse effect and usually put the audience on guard against his enemy's further efforts. The point has been applied summarily to early PWD attempts to promote dissension, by Martin F. Herz, chief leaflet writer:

Divisive propaganda—which our side attempted as regards German Army and SS, or field soldiers and Nazi party—nearly always was a failure when attempted by white media. Reason: the motivation of the enemy is too obvious.

With the German audience that PWD faced in 1944–45, this factor was especially important. What may be called the "propaganda case history of the target," a factor whose importance has not been explicitly recognized by students of propaganda, illustrates the point. The German soldiers and civilians to whom PWD spoke were people who had grown up with the legend that Allied propaganda (assisted by a "stab in the back" from the home front) had lost them World War I. Now, in World War II, the same enemy again directed its propaganda against the Germans, in greater quantity and with improved techniques. Further, the Goebbels machine had thoroughly diabolized Allied intentions toward the Germans, in advance of any statements PWD might make. Clearly, a thick layer of skepticism separated PWD from its German target. In these circumstances, PWD had little recourse other than to a systematic factualism, the *sachliche Darstellung* (matter-of-fact presentation) of which Germans are reputed to be particularly fond.

Indirection was, of course, a technique by which PWD made facts serve its purpose. The historian of 12th AG, as usual, puts the matter plainly:

The *Frontpost* never lost sight of the fact that they were propagandists first and journalists afterwards. In other words, they did not regard it as their function merely to supply the German troops with news, but to score propaganda points through the printing of news. The propaganda points to be scored were all on the same counting board: the inevitability of the German defeat, hopelessness of further resistance, and consequent desirability (for the Germans) of early surrender. Along this line, the PWD attack on German morale was drawn. Whatever the starting point, this was the line to which all PWD themes returned.

The importance of this unified line of attack can be seen by comparison with that of World War I. Dr. George C. Bruntz, an historian of Allied propaganda in World War I, has classified its output in the following five types:

(1) enlightenment
(2) despair
(3) hope
(4) particularistic
(5) revolutionary

In World War II, as indicated earlier, PWD eliminated all revolutionary propaganda, largely on the basis of Allied war policy (unconditional surrender) and target intelligence, i.e., no usable German revolutionists were available. Particularistic propaganda was eliminated on the same basis, i.e., separatist sentiment was neither strong nor usable. Propaganda of hope was eliminated on the basis of Allied policy, i.e., unconditional surrender and subsequent Allied military government. Propaganda of enlightenment, in the limited sense of propaganda which makes use of accurate factual information, was abundant. Whatever the function of enlightenment in World War I, however, its intent in World War II was not to enlighten but to cause despair. The propaganda of despair, in Dr. Bruntz's term, was in fact the inclusive category of PWD output in the final period of World War II.

Essay and Filmography
By William Murphy

World War II Propaganda Films

D uring both world wars, film was considered a potent propaganda weapon. German Chief of Staff Erich Ludendorff, writing in 1917, said: "The war has demonstrated the superiority of the photograph and the film as means of information and persuasion." George Creel, chairman of the United States Committee on Public Information, a World War I agency charged with releasing government information about the war, said that motion pictures could play a role equal to that of the written or spoken word. V. I. Lenin spoke of film's role in the Bolshevik Revolution, stating that it would be the most important of the arts. In other times of crisis—the Great Depression, the Spanish Civil War, and World War II—film became further imbued with politics. Its power to persuade uncritical audiences made it a convenient tool for propagandizing large numbers of people. All the nations involved in World War II relied on documentary film not only for propaganda but also for information and instruction, as well as for scientific, record, and legal purposes. Of more concern is that films were used to identify wartime objectives and give military and civilian views a sense of national purpose. The extent to which they succeeded varied from country to country.

BRITAIN

Great Britain, due to ten years of prior experience in documentary films, was better prepared than any other country to use the medium in World War II. The modern documentary, in fact, emerged in Britain between 1929 and 1939 under the leadership of John Grierson, Stephen Tallents, and Alberto Cavalcanti. Their remarkably precise ideas were put into practice in films for the Empire Marketing Board and the Government Post Office Film Unit. Through this work, a school of film makers was trained who believed in documentary film more as an instrument of social and civic education than as an art form. As their subjects they chose the ostensibly mundane, commonplace, and ordinary, particularly the activities of British industries and trades and the worker in his everyday role. *Nightmail* (1936), a documentary about the nightly work inside a mail train, summed up much of the documentary's accomplishment in this period, especially by its vigorous experimentation with sound, music, and narration.

The outbreak of war in late 1939 offered a golden opportunity to British documentary film makers. Alberto Cavalcanti, head of the GPO Film Unit, almost immediately seized the chance to make *First Days* (1939), which recorded the calm determination of Londoners during the first days of the war. The British Government, however, was slow to take advantage of the talent it had accumulated these past years, and slower still to evolve a national policy for the use of film. In 1940 the Ministry of Information, which was assigned responsibility for government film production, took charge of the GPO Film Unit, later named the Crown Film Unit.

Gradually films began to appear which looked inward toward the behavior and character of the British rather than outward toward the enemy. Continuing in the vein of the 1930s, they focused on the everyday lives of ordinary people, but this time addressed themselves to the stresses and anxieties of full-scale war. These films were best exemplified by Humphrey Jennings' *London Can Take It* (1940), *Listen to Britain* (1941), and *Fires Were Started* (1943). All three films highlight the dangers and tensions of life under the blitz, which makes them dramatic and exciting as documentaries, but inevitably they show resoluteness and determination, dignity and indignation, the propaganda points to be imparted to the viewer.

There was less pressure to persuade in these and other films because the war was so close. When the enemy's aggressive intentions were visible in the streets, elaborate explanations for the causes of the war were not necessary. In documentaries about the courage of firemen and civil defense wardens Britons were told what to do without having to be told why.

Films which showed actual confrontation with the enemy inspired confidence in Britain's ability to defend herself against Germany. *The Lion Has Wings* (1940) and *Squadron 992* (1940) affirmed the adequacy of Britain's air defenses, particularly the effectiveness of the RAF against the Luftwaffe in 1940, despite great odds. *Men of the Lightship* (1940) and *Western Approaches* (1944), two stories of rescue and survival, made personal sacrifice a common value of the war. Even in documentaries about military operations, human values were stressed over tactical ones. *Target for Tonight* (1942), a film about the planning and execution of a typical RAF bombing raid over Germany, showed events through the eyes of the men involved. Similarly, *Desert Victory* (1943) may be the best military campaign documentary of the war because it achieves a rare balance between the panorama of the battlefield and the values of the soldiers.

UNITED STATES

The circumstances of war had much to do with documentary film's acceptance in the United States. Despite the artistic success of Robert Flaherty's *Nanook of the North* in 1922, his film did not herald a new film movement the way John Grierson's *Drifters* (1929) later did in Britain. *Nanook* was followed by a few semidocumentaries like *Grass* (1925) and *Chang* (1927), which attempted to combine fiction techniques and documentary methods by making the most of exotic locales. Subsequently feature films like *I Am a Fugitive From a Chain Gang* (1932) and *Our Daily Bread* (1934) dealt with social issues in a realistic manner, but used actors and were based on contrived plots. *March of Time*, the monthly screen magazine which first appeared in February, 1935, stimulated further interest in documentary film, though its style was only slightly more sophisticated than the newsreels produced in the United States since 1911.

In 1936 the federal government released its first modern documentary, *The Plow That Broke the Plains*, directed by Pare Lorentz for the Resettlement Administration of the Department of Agriculture. A classic piece of Americana, Lorentz' film dramatized the causes and effects of the Dust Bowl crisis. The following year he made *The River* for the Farm Security Administration, again revealing man's abuse of his natural environment. The film explained how the federal government would correct these abuses and harness the Mississippi River system for the benefit of all. *The River*'s powerful orchestration of images, words, and music made it an enduring classic of American documentary. With the success of these two films behind him, Lorentz attempted to institutionalize documentary film making within the federal government. He was appointed director of the U.S. Film Service, established by President Roosevelt in 1938, and set high standards for government films by enlisting the talents of such outstanding film makers as Robert Flaherty

and Joris Ivens. But the films which Lorentz produced and directed drew too much attention and controversy in an era when the Hollywood industry and many congressmen felt that the government should not be making films at all. More importantly, these films could be identified with the public relations aspect of New Deal programs which had met much antipathy in Congress. Two years after the inception of the Film Service, Congress refused to vote funds for its continuation. The legislative branch showed its fear of documentary film as a propaganda tool, regardless of whose ends it might serve. This fear still persists, embodied in the legislation which prohibits the domestic showing of U.S. Information Agency films. During the war Lorentz, perhaps the country's best documentary film maker, was assigned to the Army Air Forces' Air Transport Command, where his considerable talent was largely wasted in aerial photography and the production of flight-route films for pilot training.

Outside the government, prewar American documentary film was politically to the left, in sharp opposition to the *March of Time* and the more conservative newsreels of the major film studios. Under the sponsorship of a group of American writers including Lillian Hellman, Archibald MacLeish, John Dos Passos, and Ernest Hemingway, Ivens made *The Spanish Earth* (1937), a pro-Loyalist film about the Spanish Civil War. A year later, with American capital, he made the *Four Hundred Million*, which backed the Chinese in their war against the Japanese invaders. The productions of Frontier Films, another group engaged in politics, supported unionism and condemned fascism abroad. Hollywood wanted little or no part of these controversial, often crude, and unpolished films.

The opening stages of World War II were filmed by independent documentary film makers, who brought the war to American screens. Herbert Kline's and Alexander Hammid's *Crisis* (1939) showed the German takeover of the Sudetenland as a demonstration of Nazi violence and a warning to Americans of things to come. Likewise, Kline's *Lights Out in Europe* (1940) showed calculated German attacks on Polish civilians, and Julien Bryan's *Siege* (1939), filmed from the rooftops of Warsaw, portrayed the destruction of the city by the Germans. In the United States films like the newsreel compilation *The*

Last Stronghold (1940) argued for a defense build-up and preparation. Perhaps the best known of these preparation films was *The Ramparts We Watch* (1940), directed by Louis de Rochemont for *March of Time*. A hybrid feature-documentary echoing the position of the *Time* publishing empire, it drew simplistic parallels between the United States' entry into World War I and events of the present crisis. It concluded with lengthy extracts from the German film *Feuertaufe* (*Baptism of Fire*, 1940) as a warning of Nazi intentions, one of the first instances in the United States of reusing German footage for anti-Nazi propaganda. Additionally, the major film studios turned out several anti-Nazi feature films between 1939 and 1941. *Confessions of a Nazi Spy* (1939), *A Dispatch from Reuters* (1940), and *Manhunt* (1941) were inflammatory enough to come under the scrutiny of a subcommittee of the Senate Interstate Commerce Committee investigating the alleged dissemination of war propaganda.

German films like *Feuertaufe* and *Sieg im Westen* (*Victory in the West*, 1941) circulated throughout the United States as intimidation rather than information. Distributed by UFA Films Inc. of New York, which was controled by the Reich's Propaganda Ministry, these films were enthusiastically welcomed in some of the German-American neighborhoods and by German societies and bunds.

When war came to the United States, the military departments quickly drew upon a major portion of the Hollywood film community. Among the well-known makers of entertainment films inducted into military service were Anatole Litvak, Gregg Toland, John Huston, and William Wyler, who transferred some of the "glamour" of the film industry to warfare. Actually, John Ford and Frank Capra, recruited by the navy and army respectively, had been promised commissions before the war and were only waiting to be called into service. Just as in peacetime, the Hollywood community, or the portion now in uniform, remained isolated from experienced documentary film makers, many of whom were hired by the newly established Office of War Information. So, without a clear conception of documentary film's technique or purposes, without the experience of depicting a reality not controled by the camera, nor of working with non–professional actors, entertainment film makers in uniform assumed the major responsibility for bringing the war to the screen, guided mainly by their instinctive understanding of the medium.

Hollywood directors profoundly affected the style of American military documentaries. The more dramatic color films, released for theatrical distribution, were expertly edited to move emotions rather than convey information. John Ford's *The Battle of Midway* (1942) told precious little of how the United States Navy defeated the Japanese fleet. For action, Ford chose to emphasize the Japanese attack on Midway Island while the main battle took place between the ships and planes of both sides far at sea. The portrayal of the rescued American flyers, also featured in the film, was drenched in patriotic sentimentality, with no information furnished about what they had been through or had accomplished. Ford shows instead an idealized relationship between pilots and their friends and relatives back home.

Where the German film makers felt they must have factual footage to support their narrations—even the most outlandish assertions—American film makers from the entertainment industry were cavalier toward photographic authenticity. The Office of Strategic Service's *December 7th*, produced and directed by John Ford and Gregg Toland (the cameraman for *Citizen Kane*), liberally intercut shots of the Pearl Harbor attack with studiolike scenes. Dramatized situations, the use of professional actors, syrupy music, and color photography made the transition from entertainment to documentary easier for audiences accustomed to lighter fare.

As a director John Huston made the most successful shift from entertainment films to wartime documentary. Each of the three films, based on original shooting controled by him, presented the human experience of war: *Report from the Aleutians* (1944), the experience of combat airmen in a forgotten corner of the Pacific; *San Pietro* (1944), the bitter fighting and high casualties in one small Italian mountain village; and *Let There Be Light* (1946), the mental casualties of the fighting men.

No other country felt the need to explain the war in the moral terms evident in American films. *Prelude to War* (1943), the introduction to the important "Why We Fight" series of military orientation films, divides the world into good and evil ideologies. Democracy, the former, is rooted in the work ethic, individualism, and free elections; fascism, the latter, in fear, conformity, and dictatorship. According to *Prelude to War,* the aggressive acts of Germany, Italy, and Japan were not the only reasons why the United States went to war. Just as important was the despicable structure of fascist societies in which the faceless masses gave up their individual freedom to ruthless and calculating dictators bent on world conquest. Another film in the "Why We Fight" series, *War Comes To America* (1944), inculcated pride in the American political and economic system and cast doubt on its future achievements in the event of Axis victories in Europe and Asia. If isolationism was a factor in the prewar politics, such films laid it permanently to rest.

The bulk of American military war films, though, can best be characterized by their matter-of-fact, almost reportorial approach. These films were devoid of emotion, even when reporting on deeply moving subjects like the bombing of Hiroshima and Nagasaki and the liberation of Nazi concentration camps. But they should be distinguished from incentive or propaganda films that attempted to motivate audiences by teaching lessons of politics and morality.

The Office of War Information was the major civilian producer of documentary films for domestic and overseas propaganda. To its ranks gravitated many of the experienced documentary film makers and administrators who first became interested in the social possibilities of the medium during the 1930s. Lowell Mellett and Arch Mercey, attempting to continue Lorentz' work, supervised the production of films for the OWI's Domestic Bureau. But here too they encountered stiff opposition from Congress and the Hollywood industry. With the Domestic Bureau's budget reduced to a ridiculous sum, its motion picture production ceased in July, 1943, right in the middle of the war.

Because its films were made for foreign audiences, the OWI Overseas Branch encountered less hostility from the industry, Congress, and other bureaus. The film makers recruited were among the best available: Alexander Hammid, Willard Van Dyke, Irving Lerner, Henwar Rodakiewicz, and others. Their quiet and thoughtful films captured the often overlooked virtues of the American landscape and people. There is little social criticism in *The Cummington Story, The Town,* or *Tuesday in November,* only tolerance and democratic government, work and achievement, answers to fascist propaganda about the United States.

SOVIET UNION

Persuasion and politics were the essence of Soviet films even before World War II. Motion pictures, according to Lenin, had to spread the new ideology of the Bolshevik Revolution. In 1919, therefore, the Seventh Congress of the Communist Party included film among the arts that had to promote communism, and in August of that year Soviet motion picture production was nationalized, bringing it under the scrutiny of the party and state.

The 1920s in the Soviet Union were years of enormous artistic energy and experimentation from which the international documentary film could benefit, especially within the realm of propaganda. Dziga Vertov, one of the most important film makers of this period, was among the first to exploit newsreel footage to formulate analyses of current events. This approach is exemplified in the series *Kinopravda (Cinema Truth),* 1922–25. Sergei Eisenstein, the leading theoretician of Soviet cinema, re-created historical events of key interest to the new government. In *Strike* (1924) and *Ten Days That Shook the World* (1927–28) he demonstrated that conflict is the basis of film montage or editing. He recognized the shot as the basic unit of the film, and it was the arrangement of shots, he said, along the lines of dialectical reasoning by which the film maker could make a precise visual statement to the viewer. The use of counterpoint in the Odessa Steps sequence of *Potemkin* (1925) is Eisenstein's most celebrated example of montage. Thus Eisenstein established the use of thesis and antithesis in film editing.

The most fundamental contribution of the Soviet film makers to films of persuasion was their demonstration of how film could foster a social consciousness. They severed the link that tied film to entertainment and escapism. The masses and the common man became their heroes, and social criticism their objective.

But even their sincere communist films were rejected as "formalist" and bourgeois avant-garde art by stolid commissars of the Communist Party, who preferred more conventional story films with sympathetic individuals for audience identification. Such films as Alexander Dovzhenko's *Earth*, a romantic tribute to nature, were found inimical to economic reconstruction. By the 1930s all of the major social realists of the prior decade were out of favor. Documentaries were largely restricted to nature studies, travelogues, and biographies, while feature films dealt with political subjects like the civil war, collectivization, and the Moscow trials. The feature film, in addition, was a better reflection of international events in Stalinist Russia. *Volochayevsk Days* (1938) and *Alexander Nevsky* (1938) evinced strong national feelings against the Japanese and Germans. Several other antifascist features were made in the late 1930s, but were taken out of circulation after the signing of the Molotov-von Ribbentrop Pact of August 23, 1939. After the German invasion of the Soviet Union, needless to say, they were recirculated, and more antifascist films were produced with greater vehemence.

World War II, otherwise an unqualified disaster for the Soviet Union, had a salutory effect on the Soviet documentary, which took on greater importance than the theatrical feature. Directors long forgotten were put into service making documentaries, where there seemed to be more room for creativity and less censorship than in the complicated production of features. Attendance at documentary film showings was high, owing to the insatiable demand for news from the massive front. Interesting beginnings were *Mannerheim Line* (1940), which presented the Russian view of the winter war against Finland, and *Liberation* (1940), which showed military conditions in the western Ukraine before the German invasion.

The invasion of the Soviet Union caused the retreat and dispersal of the Soviet film industry from Moscow eastward to the farthest corners of the country. The Central and Ukranian Newsreel Studios became centers of war film production. To a very great extent, film production was based on the compilation technique, for rarely did a director have the opportunity to go into the field to direct his cameramen. Left to their own devices, Soviet combat cameramen, whose losses were high, sent footage to a central production point where it was edited into completed films.

The celebrated defense of Moscow was portrayed in films for American distribution. Serving as an example to the world of Soviet resistance against the German invaders, the *Defeat of the German Armies near Moscow* was remade with an English sound track and released in the United States by Republic Pictures as *Moscow Strikes Back* (1942). Other Soviet films reworked by American film makers, such as *Our Russian Front* (1941), served to build the cause of Russo-American friendship. Even Soviet newsreels in English were released for this purpose.

If there are common themes running through Soviet war documentaries they are the violation of the homeland, Nazi brutality, and the stubborn persistence and triumph of the Russian people despite great difficulties. The films about the seiges of Moscow, Leningrad, and Stalingrad, turned into routs by the Russian defenders, have a similar thematic structure. So too, the documentaries of Dovzhenko, whose idealized love for his homeland shows in each of his films about the fighting in the Ukraine. Each Soviet film had to end in victory or at least present the portent of victory. The success of the German armies was consistently minimized. German prisoners were displayed in long tracking shots along with tons of destroyed German equipment. The wake of the German armies consistently revealed the shocking evidence of Nazi atrocities committed against the peoples of Eastern Europe. And just as British and American films judiciously avoided the subject of communism, Russian films designed for export rarely mentioned it, carefully guarding as well their statements about democracy and capitalism. Such was the expediency of war.

GERMANY

Josef Goebbels, the German minister of enlightenment and propaganda, had a compulsive interest in the motion picture as an instrument of persuasion for government and war. He was largely responsible for the nationalization of the German film industry after the establishment of the Film Office in 1933. It has been said that he received his inspiration for film propaganda from the success of Russian revolutionary films like *Battleship Potemkin* (1925) and *The End of St. Petersburg* (1927), even though the sincere communist intention of these films could not pose a greater anathema to Nazi power.

The aims of documentary film in Germany were essentially political: to glorify Hitler's personal image and disseminate Nazi ideology. Even the most innocuous

Kulturfilm was intended to help the propaganda ministry disseminate a Nazi view of German history and culture. The Nazi party was quick to perceive the role of film as an instrument of political enhancement. One of its first sponsored films, *Hitlers Flug über Deutschland* (*Hitler's Flight over Germany,* 1932) showed Hitler's travels through Germany during the election campaign of 1932. Other election films followed.

It also became common to film the massive annual party rallies at Nuremburg and use the resultant films for showings throughout Germany. Leni Riefenstahl, a former actress turned director, directed the rally films of 1933, *Sieg des Glaubens* (*Victory of Faith*), and of 1934, *Triumph des Willens* (*Triumph of the Will*). Because of the personal control of Riefenstahl as an artist, the latter film was made despite Goebbels, who appeared to have a bitter hatred or jealousy of the director. *Triumph of the Will,* with good reason, is the most outstanding propaganda film of this whole era. In addition to being a brilliant visualization of the monster rally, it captures a state of mind, revealing what Hitler and Nazism meant to many Germans. In the well-known opening scenes Hitler descends on the banner-covered city like a god from Olympus, and Nazism is shown rooted deeply in Nuremburg's medieval past. As used by the Allies, footage from *Triumph of the Will* showed the surrender of individual freedom to aggressive dictatorship.

German documentaries produced at the outbreak of war were planned entirely for effect and betray a naive faith in the power of film to persuade. So long as factual footage was used, the commentator could say anything and it would be believed. Perhaps these films were successful within Germany because they were the only exposure Germans had to the events of the war. But no one outside Germany could take seriously, for example, the wild accusations of Polish aggression against Germany in *Feuertaufe* (*Baptism of Fire,* 1940). That such a film would be intended for use abroad indicates the utter provincialism of the Nazi regime. Nevertheless, epic military campaign films like this one and *Sieg im Westen* (*Victory in the West,* 1941) were indeed calculated for their impact on the outside world, particularly potential adversaries of Germany. Together they displayed the deadly accuracy of the Luftwaffe and the devastating

speed of mechanized warfare. German tactics were shown to be as flawless as a mathematical formula, while the enemy was shown demoralized, if not degenerate, and unable to resist German attack.

The superior surface qualities of Nazi films—the use of music, rhythmic editing, light values, and camera angles—stunned the emotions and obscured the thinness of the content. Underneath, Nazi film propaganda was fierce, dedicated to war, and intellectually contemptible of the viewer. The hatred reeking from *Der Ewige Jude* (*The Eternal Jew,* 1940), a documentary about the "inferiority of Jews," is astounding even in an era of hateful films. In such films the documentary medium was not used to explore reality but to assert official positions on "national problems." Like Nazi authority itself, the assertions lacked valid demonstrations or explanation.

JAPAN

The Japanese failed to exploit the full potential of actuality or documentary films as a propaganda weapon. Japan's wartime films lacked real information and made little effort toward a documentary style. Not photographing the attack on Pearl Harbor in greater detail was a singular tactical error. The surviving footage, used later in newsreels and documentaries, failed to give a good idea of the damage. The entertainment feature, rigidly controled by the government from script to distribution, served as the main conduit for propaganda.

A film as early as *Japan in Time of Emergency* (1933), sponsored by the war ministry, pointed to the infiltration of Western cultural imperialism into traditional Japanese society. This was a theme common to Japanese films later made for occupied countries. *Victory Song of the Orient* (1942), certainly the most ambitious of these films, dealt with racism toward Asiatic peoples and the Westernization of Asian cultures. The alternative offered in such films was a place in Japan's Greater East Asia Co-Prosperity Sphere, where the newly independent nations would share Japan's wealth exclusive of Western influence. *To Establish a New Order in East Asia* (1939) and *Dawn of Freedom* (1941) are other important examples.

A greater number of films were made for the China campaign, such as *Japan Advancing toward the North* (1934) and *Hammer Blows against China* (1937). *Why Defend China?* (1938), later released in English, blames

Japan's invasion of China on the "aggressive actions of the Chinese nationalists and on the underlying threat of the Comintern and Red imperialists." Like the German film *Feuertaufe*, it is a startling document justifying the invasion of one country by another. *Paradise in New Manchuria*, part of the China campaign propaganda, portrays this region as a rich economic area enjoying the benefits of Japanese administration.

Battles of Hawaii and the Malay Sea (1942) and *Battles on the Indian Ocean* (1942) were two fairly successful naval campaign films, but the credibility of the former was weakened by intercutting footage of battle scenes created with miniature models in the studio.

FILMOGRAPHY

The accompanying filmography consists of selected documentary or actuality films produced prior to and during World War II. Those produced during the 1930s show events that led up to the war. With a few exceptions, war-related documentaries made after 1945 are not included, even though they may appear to be based on authentic footage. Their points of view, so important for the study of documentary as propaganda, are not genuinely contemporary with the war. Nor are theatrical films (with one exception) included, although they are valuable for the wartime viewpoint and propaganda they contain. The films selected give the appearance of being factual and have the primary objective of informing rather than entertaining.

The selections, moreover, represent a small and perhaps unfair sampling of the thousands of films produced during the war. The larger, more powerful participants—Britain, the Soviet Union, Japan, the United States, and Germany—have received the greatest attention, but films from Italy, Canada, and China are also included. No effort has been made to include serial items like newsreels or screen magazines, produced in each of the major countries. Where possible the name of the director or producer is included, and a brief description of each film.

Many of the listed films are available for study in major film archives such as the National Archives and the Library of Congress in Washington, D.C.; the Museum of Modern Art in New York; the Imperial War Museum and the National Film Archive in London; and the Bundesarchiv in Koblenz, West Germany.

BRITAIN

Airscrew, Shell Oil. Arthur Elton, prod., Grahame Thorp, dir., 1940. An incentive film aimed at British industrial workers; illustrates the manufacture of metal airplane propellers.

Battle of the Books, Ministry of Information. Paul Rotha, prod., Jack Chambers, dir., 1941.

Cameramen at War, Realist Film Unit for the Ministry of Information. Len Lye, prod., 1944. A brief history of the work of top cameramen in combat.

The Curse of the Swastika, Pathé. Fred Watts, prod., 1940.

Dangerous Comment, Michael Balcon, prod., 1939.

The Dawn Guard, Ministry of Information. John Boulting, prod., Ray Boulting, dir., 1941.

Desert Victory, Army Film and Photograph Unit and the RAF Film Production Unit. David MacDonald, prod., Roy Boulting, dir., 1943. The British 8th Army campaign against Rommel's Afrika Korps, from El Alamein to Tripoli.

A Diary of Timothy, Crown Film Unit, Basil Wright, prod., Humphrey Jennings, dir., E. M. Forster, script, 1945. The story of a boy born into war and the conditions in which he and other children could expect to grow up.

Dustbin Parade, Ministries of Supply and Information. John Taylor, prod., John Halas and Joy Batchelor, animators; 1942.

The Eighty Days, Crown Film Unit. Humphrey Jennings, prod. and dir., Edward R. Murrow, commentary, 1944.

Fires Were Started, Crown Film Unit. Ian Dalrymple, prod., Humphrey Jennings, dir. and script, 1943. The excitement, tension, and suspense of civil defense during the London blitz.

The First Days, Government Post Office Film Unit. Alberto Cavalcanti, prod.; Harry Watt, dir, 1939. Interprets the atmosphere of London during September 1939, emphasizing calm determination, a sense of unity, and common purpose.

From the Four Corners, Denham and Pinewood for the Ministry of Information. A. Havelock-Allen, prod. and dir., 1941.

Germany Calling, Spectator Productions. Charles Ridley, prod., 1941. Excerpts from *Triumph of the Will* and other films of the Nuremberg rallies reedited to the tune of "Doing the Lambeth Walk."

The Heart of Britain, Government Post Office Film Unit for the Ministry of Information. Humphrey Jennings, dir., 1941.

Hitler Listens, Army Kinema Korps, 1944.

Kill or Be Killed, Ministry of Information for the War Office. Len Lye, dir., 1942. An instruction film for unarmed combat.

The Lion Has Wings. Royal Treasury. Alexander Korda, prod., 1940. The courage of the RAF pitted against great odds.

Listen to Britain, Crown Film Unit. Ian Dalrymple, prod., Humphrey Jennings and Stuart McAllister, dir., 1942.

London Can Take It, Crown Film Unit. Harry Watt and Humphrey Jennings, dir., 1940. The dignity of Londoners during one night in the first London blitz.

Men of the Lightship, Crown Film Unit. Alberto Cavalcanti, prod., David MacDonald, dir., 1940. Reconstructs the German attack on an unarmed lightship, whose survivors must struggle to reach land.

A New Fire Bomb, Shell Film Unit for the Ministries of Home Security and Information. Edgar Anstey, prod., Napier Beu, dir., 1942.

Newspaper Train, Realist for the Ministry of Information. 1941.

The Next of Kin, Ealing Studios for the Directorate of Army Kinematography. Michael Balcon, prod., Thorold Dickinson, dir., 1942.

Night Shift, Ministries of Supply and Information. Paul Rotha, prod., Jack Chambers, dir., 1942. The night shift of women workers in an ordnance factory.

Ordinary People, Crown Film Unit for the Ministry of Information. J. B. Holmes and Jack Lee, dir., 1941.

The Rape of Czechoslovakia, Paul Rotha. Frank H. Cox, prod., Jiri Weiss, dir., 1939. The German takeover of Czechoslovakia.

Salute to the Red Army, Newsreel Association for the Ministry of Information. Raymond Perris, compilation, 1943.

The Silent Village, Crown Film Unit in cooperation with the Czech Ministry of Foreign Affairs and the South Wales Miners Federation. Humphrey Jennings, dir. A memorial to the people of Lidice in the setting of a South Wales mining village.

A Soviet Village, Ministry of Information. Paul Rotha, prod., Jack Chamber, supervisor, 1944.

Spring Offensive, Government Post Office Film Unit. Alberto Gavalcanti, prod., Humphrey Jennings, dir., 1940. British farmers supply food for the homefront and for soldiers abroad.

Squadron 992, Government Post Office Film Unit for the RAF. Albert Cavalcanti, prod., Harry Watt, dir., 1940. The dramatic reconstruction of the Firth of Forth raid in the early weeks of the war; describes the defensive role of the balloon barrage.

Target for Tonight, Crown Film Unit. Ian Dalrymple, prod., Harry Watt, dir. and script, 1942. A dramatization of the courage of a British bombing crew during a raid over Germany as seen through the eyes of the men involved; shows the origin, planning, execution, and completion of a bombing run.

These Are the Men, Strand Film for the Ministry of Information. Donald Taylor, prod., Alan Osbiston, dir., Dylan Thomas, script, 1943. Sequences of *Triumph of the Will* with a propagandistic commentary.

They Also Serve, Realist Film Unit for the Ministry of Information. Ruby Grierson, dir., 1940. The role of British housewives during the war.

The True Story of Lili Marlene, Crown Film Unit. Humphrey Jennings, dir., 1944.

Tunisian Victory, Ministry of Information (Anglo-American production), 1944. The logistics of landing in darkness during the Tunisian campaign.

V-1: The Robot Bomb, Crown Film Unit, 1944.

Wales, Green Mountain, Black Mountain. Strand for the Ministry of Information. Donald Taylor, prod., John Eldridge, dir., Dylan Thomas, commentary; 1942.

We Sail at Midnight, Ministry of Information. Julian Spiro, dir., 1941. The operation of the lend-lease arrangement in supplying essential tools to a British tank factory.

Western Approaches, Crown Film Unit. Ian Dalrymple, prod., Pat Jackson, dir., 1944. U-boat drama, including a torpedoed crew, rescue, and the destruction of a submarine.

Words and Actions, British Commercial Gas Association. Edgar Anstey, prod., Max Anderson, dir., 1943.

World of Plenty, Ministry of Information. Paul Rotha, prod., dir., 1943. The effects of war on the distribution and consumption of food and the responsibility of the government to ensure the nation's nutrition.

Yellow Caesar, Ealing Studios Ltd. Michael Balcon, prod., Alberto Cavalcanti, dir., 1941. A devastating carciature of Mussolini.

Yesterday is Over Your Shoulder, Ministry of Information. Deham and Pinewood Production Co. Thorold Dicikson, prod. and dir., 1940.

CANADA

Action Stations, Canadian National Film Board. Joris Ivens, dir., 1943.

Churchill's Island, War Film Production Activities. John Grierson, dir., 1941. The overall plan for the defense of Britain, from individual action to total strategy.

Food—Weapon of Conquest, War Film Production Activities, 1942.

This is Blitz, War Film Production Activities. John Grierson, dir., 1942.

The Thousand Days, B. E. Norrish Inc. and Associated Screen Studios. Gordon Sparling, dir., 1943.

World in Action, Canadian National Film Board. John Grierson and Stuart Legg, prod. and dir. A monthly series reporting on all warfronts and the domestic scene.

CHINA

Dr. Bethune, Yehan Film Group. Wu Yin Lsien, photography; 1939. Portrays the Canadian doctor Norman Bethune with guerilla fighters of the border region.

North China is Ours, Northwest Film Co., 1939. The progress of the war against the Japanese in northwest China by the United Front; also, officers of the 8th Route (Communist) Army amid Kuomintang opponents.

Suiyuan Mongol Front, Northwest Film Co., 1935.
Yenan and the 8th Route Army, Yenan Film Group.
Yuan Mu-jih, dir., 1939.

DENMARK

The Grain is in Danger, Hagen Hasselbalch, dir., 1944.
The invasion of Denmark by the corn weevil serves as an
allegory of the German occupation.
Your Freedom is at Stake, Theodore Christensen, dir.

FRANCE

La Bataille du Rail (*Battle of the Rails*), Cooperative
Générale du Cinéma Francais. René Clement, dir. and script,
c. 1945. Railroad sabotage by the resistance during the German
occupation of France.
Journal de la Résistance (*Journal of the Resistance*),
Le Comité du Libération du Cinéma Francais, 1944.
La Tragédie de Mers-el-Kebir, Service Cinématographique
de la Marine Francaise. Jean Antoine, commentary, 1940.
Made under the German occupation.
Une et Indivisible (*One and Indivisible*), L'Office Francais
d'Information Cinématographique, 1944.

GERMANY

Adolph Hitlers Bauten (*Adolf Hitler's Public Works*),
UFA. Walter Hege, dir., 1938.
Bauten im Neuen Deutschland (*Building in the New
Germany*), Boehmer Film, 1939.
Das Buch der Deutschen (*The Germans' Book*), Tolirag
Film, 1938.
Bückebürg, Reichspropagandaleitung (RPL), 1935.
Deutsche Panzer (*German Panzer*), UFA. Walter Ruttman,
dir., 1941.
Deutschland Erwacht (*Germany Awakes*), NSDAP, 1933.
The Nazi movement up to 1933.
Dr. Todt—Berufung und Werk (*Dr. Todt—Vocation and
Work*), Hauptamt für Technik der NSDAP, 1935.
Einsatz der Jugend (*Youth in Action*), Gunther Boehnert,
dir., 1939.
Englische Krankheit (*The English Sickness*), UFA. Kurt
Stefan, dir., 1939.
Der Ewige Jude (*The Eternal Jew*), DFG. Fritz Hippler,
dir., Dr. E. Taubert, idea and commentary, 1940. The Nazi view
of the "Jewish Question."
Feldzug im Polen (*Campaign in Poland*), DFG and
Deutsche Wochenschau. Fritz Hippler, dir., 1940. A terrifying
account of the Nazi blitzkreig in Poland with an emphasis on
ground operations.
Feuertaufe (*Baptism of Fire*), Tobis, for the Reich Air
Force Ministry. Hans Bertram, dir., 1940. The German victory
over Poland through the use of air power coordinated with
ground forces.
Der Führer Schenkt den Juden Eine Stadt (*The Führer*

Gives the Jews a Town), Aktualia, Psag, for the Ministry of
Propaganda and the SS. Kurt Gerron, dir., 1944.
German Entry into Austria, 1938.
Gestern und Heute (*Yesterday and Today*), Reichs-
propagandaleitung (RPL) der NSDAP. Hans Weidemann,
dir., 1938.
Herr Roosevelt Plaudert (*Mr. Roosevelt Chats*), 1943.
Hitlers Flug über Deutschland (*Hitler's Flight over
Germany*), NSDAP, Munich, 1932. One of the first party films;
Hitler's flights over Germany during the election campaign of
1932.
Jud Süss (*Jew Süss*), Ministry of Propaganda. Viet Harlan,
dir., 1940. An anti-Semitic feature film starring Werner Kraus.
Kampfgeschwader Lutzow (*Fighter Squadron Lutzow*),
1941.
Mussolini in Deutschland (*Mussolini in Germany*),
Fox-Tonende Wochenschau, 1937.
Olympiad: Fest der Volker, Fest der Schönheit (*Olympia:
Festival of the People, Festival of Beauty*), Leni Riefenstahl,
prod. and dir., 1938. The 1936 Olympic Games in Berlin.
Rundfunk im Krieg (*Radio in War*), Lex-Film Berlin,
for the Ministry of Propaganda, 1944.
Rund um die Freiheitsstatue (*Round about the Freedom
Statue*), Deutsche Wochenschau GmbH, for the Ministry of
Propaganda, 1942.
Sieg des Glaubens (*Victory of Faith*), NSDAP, Leni
Riefenstahl, dir., 1933. The 1933 Nazi party rally at Nuremberg.
Sieg im Westen (*Victory in the West*), Filmabteilung des
Propagandaminsterium. Fritz Hippler, prod., Svend Nolan, dir.,
1941. Germany's defeat of France.
Soldaten von Morgen (*Soldiers of Tomorrow*), Deutsche
Film GmbH. Alfred Weidenmann, dir. and script, 1941.
Das Sowjetparadies (*The Soviet Paradise*),
Reichspropagandaleitung (RPL). Friedrich Albat, dir., 1943.
Supreme Court Trial of the Anti-Hitler Plotters, 1944.
A film of the trial of those accused of conspiracy in the attempted
assassination of Adolf Hitler on July 20, 1944.
Tag der Freiheit (*Day of Freedom*), Reichsparteitagfilm,
Berlin. Leni Riefenstahl, dir., 1935. A tribute to the Wehrmacht.
Triumph des Willens (*Triumph of the Will*), NSDAP. Leni
Riefenstahl, prod. and dir., 1935. A spectacular account of the
1934 Nazi party rally at Nuremberg.
Unser Führer des Reiches Wiedergeburt (*Our Führer of
the Reich's Rebirth*), NSDAP, 1934. An election film.

ITALY

Battle of the Ionian Sea, 1940. The Italian air and naval
campaign against the British in the Ionian Sea and
Mediterranean areas.
The First Blow Against the British Empire, 1940. The
Italian campaign against the British in Somaliland and France.

Four Days of Battle, Instituto Nazionale LUCE, 1940. The Italian invasion of France.

Path of Heroes, c. 1936. The campaign in Ethiopia.

JAPAN

Battles of Hawaii and the Malay Sea (also called *War at Sea*), Toho Productions, 1942. Documentarylike style, but contains reenacted scenes and battles staged with models.

Battles on the Indian Ocean (also called *Gochin*), 1942. Filmed during a Japanese submarine cruise mission.

The Capture of Burma, 1943.

Dawn of Freedom, Toho Productions, 1942. The Philippines under United States rule; shows the conquest by Japan and the benefits of sharing in the Great East Asian Co-Prosperity Sphere.

Hammer Blows Against China, 1937. Newsreel reports of Japanese forces in China.

Japan Advancing to the North, 1934. The Japanese forces in China.

Japan in Time of Emergency, Japanese War Ministry and the Osaka Mainichi Newspaper Publishing Co., 1933. A film about the military and spiritual strength of the Japanese people; criticizes Western culture in Japanese society.

Malaya Taken, 1943.

Occupation of Sumatra, 1943.

Paradise of New Manchuria, no date. Manchuria as a beautiful, rich agriculture region with industry, modern cities, and a prosperous citizenry enjoying the benefits of work, education, and leisure.

Reconstructed China and Cooperation, North China Film Co., 1939.

To Establish a New Order in East Asia, Manchurian Motion Picture Assn., 1939.

Victory Song of the Orient, Sampaguita Pictures Inc., 1942. The Japanese conquest of the Philippines.

Why Defend China?, International Cinema Assn. of Japan, 1938. Blames Japan's invasion of China on the "aggressive action" of the Chinese Nationalists and on the underlying threat by the Comintern and "Red imperialism."

NETHERLANDS

The Last Shot, Ministry of Information. John Ferno, dir. and photography, no date.

POLAND

Battle of Lenino, Polish Army Military Film Unit, 1943.

Tale of a City: Warsaw, Polish Film Unit in Great Britain, 1944.

SOVIET UNION

The Battle for the Ukraine, Central Newsreel Studios. Alexander Dovzhenko, supervisor, Julia Solntseva and L. Bodik, dir.

The Battle of Vitebsk, Central Documentary Film Studio, 1944. With a staggering loss of human life, a Russian offensive liberates Vitebsk, a city held by the Germans for more than three years.

Berlin, Central Newsreel Studio. Yuli Raizman and Y. Svilova, dir., 1945. The campaign for Berlin, its surrender and occupation.

A Day of War, Central Newsreel Studio. Mikhail Slutsky, dir., 1942. Footage from all fronts as photographed on a single day—June 13, 1942.

The Defeat of Japan, Documentary Film Studio. Alexander Zarkhi and Josef Heifitz, dir., 1945.

The Defeat of the German Armies Near Moscow, Leonid Varlamov and Ilya Kopalin, dir., 1942. The role of civilians in the defense of the city, the battle outside Moscow, and the Red offensive which captured enemy-held towns. Released through Republic Pictures in the United States as *Moscow Strikes Back*, narrated by Edward G. Robinson.

Defense of Moscow, Central Newsreel Studio, Artkino, 1941. Serves as an example to the world of Soviet resistance to the German armies, whose forces are routed.

Estonian Earth, V. Byelayev, dir., 1940.

The Fight for our Soviet Ukraine, Central and Ukranian Newsreel Studios. Alexander Dovzhenko, Supervisor; Yulia Solntseva and Yakov Avdeyenko, dir., 1943. A tranquil agricultural region is invaded by the German armies.

Komsomols, Lydia Stepanova and Sergei Gurov, dir., 1943. The role of the Komsomols (Soviet Youth) in Russian history since 1918, including their role in the war.

Leningrad in Combat, Leningrad Studio. Roman Karmen et al., dir., 1942.

Liberated France, Documentary Film Studio. Sergei Yutkevich, editor; 1944. Allied footage on the liberation of France, recut by the Russians.

Liberation, Kiev Studio. Alexander Dovzhenko, dir.; Yulia Solntseva, co-dir., 1940. Conditions in the Western Ukraine and Western Byelorussia in September 1939, when Red troops moved up following the German attack on Poland.

The Liberation of Czechoslovakia, Ilya Kopalin and Pera Atasheva, dir., 1944. Reconstructs Czech history as an independent nation and its fate under Nazi occupation.

Mannerheim Line, V. Belayev, dir., 1940. The winter war against Finland.

Men of the Black Sea, 1942. Russian naval and ground operations against the Germans in the Black Sea region.

Our Russian Front, Russian War Relief Fund Inc., Artkino. Joris Ivens and Lewis Milestone, prod., Walter Huston, commentator, 1941. A compilation based on Soviet combat footage.

The People's Avengers, Central Newsreel Studios. V. Belayev, dir., 1943.

The Red Army, 1940.

Red Tanks, Lenfilm Studio, Artkino. Z. Drapkin and R. Maiman, dir. and writers; 1944. A staged film in which a daring Soviet tank corps rallies to the defense of the nation and thwarts the enemy.

The Siege of Leningrad, Lenin Newsreel Studios, 1942. A picture of life in the surrounded city of Leningrad; the underlying theme is Soviet determination for survival.

Stalingrad, Central Newsreel Studios. Leonid Varlamov, editor; Smirnov, Music, 1943. From the German air attacks and close fighting within the city to Field Marshall von Paulus' surrender of German forces on January 31, 1943.

To the Danube, Central and Ukranian Newsreel Studios, Poselsky and I. Kopalin, dir., 1940.

Toward an Armistice with Finland, Central Documentary Studio. Yuli Raizman, dir., 1944. Soviet-Finnish relations, 1939–44.

Ukraine in Flames, Central Newsreel and Kiev Studios. Alexander Dovzhenko and Yulia Solntseva, dir., 1945. The 1944 Soviet offensive in the Ukraine.

UNITED STATES

Action at Anguar. Signal Corps, 1945. The invasion and capture of Anguar Island by the 81st "Wildcat" Infantry Division in its first battle.

America's Hidden Weapon, Warner Bros. for the Office of War Information. William McGann, dir., 1944. Farmers and victory gardeners supply increased agricultural needs.

Appointment in Tokyo, Signal Corps in cooperation with the Army Air Force and the Department of the Navy, 1945. The war against Japan (1942–45) from the Japanese capture of Corregidor to Japan's surrender.

Army-Navy Screen Magazine, Signal Corps. Leonard Spiegelglass, prod., 1943–45. Entertainment and war news with a magazine format, designed for the serviceman.

Attack: The Battle for New Britain, Signal Corps, 1944. Explains the strategy of the New Britain campaign and comments on jungle life.

At the Front in North Africa, Signal Corps. Darryl F. Zanuck, prod., 1943. Covers the Allied landing in Algeria through the defeat of the Germans and Italians in Tunisia.

Autobiography of a Jeep, Office of War Information. Joseph Krumgold, prod. and dir., 1943. The story of the design, manufacture, and use of the jeep, humorously told from the jeep's point of view.

The Battle for the Marianas, Warner Bros. for the Marine Corps, 1943. A campaign documentary.

The Battle of Midway, Department of the Navy. John Ford, dir., 1942. The first American naval victory in the Pacific; centers on the island attack and the rescue of downed flyers.

Baptism of Fire, War Department, 1943. An acted film

which recreates the apprehension of a soldier's first combat experience; shows how fears and anxieties are channeled into murderous aggressive instincts.

Bomber, Office of Emergency Management. Carl Sandburg, script, 1941. Details the usefulness and effectiveness of the B-26 medium bomber.

Brought to Action, Office of Strategic Services with the Department of the Navy, 1944. The Seventh Fleet on guard in the Gulf of Leyte in the Philippines.

Challenge to Democracy, War Relocation Authority, 1943. The forced relocation and internment of Japanese-Americans.

China Strikes Back, Frontier Films. Jay Jeyda, Irving Lerner, and Sydney Myers, 1937. The Red Army campaign against the Japanese in Shenshi.

Conquest by the Clock, RKO-Pathé. Slavko Vorkapich, dir., 1943. The importance of time in the production of war goods.

Crisis, Herbert Kline and Alexander Hamid, 1939. The fifth column in the Sudetenland; warning in America of things to come; Nazi violence against Czechs and German democrats.

The Cummington Story, Office of War Information. Irving Lerner, prod.; Helen Grayson and Larry Madison, dir. and script; Aaron Copland, music. An acted film depicting the accepting of war refugees in a New England town.

Dangerous Pennies, Office of Price Administration, 1945.

December 7, Office of Strategic Services. John Ford, prod., Gregg Toland, dir., 1942. A staged film intercut with documentary footage.

The Enemy Japan—Dream of Empire, Signal Corps, 1945. The Japanese expansion during the 1930s and World War II. Shows the use of occupied countries for the supply of raw materials.

The Enemy Japan—The Land, March of Time for the Department of the Navy, 1943. Joseph Grew, former U.S. Ambassador to Japan, describes Japanese land, agriculture, and industry.

The Enemy Japan—The People, March of Time for the Department of the Navy, 1943. Grew describes the effect of Shintoism and the samurai code on the Japanese psychology.

The Fighting Lady, Department of the Navy. Louis de Rochemont, prod. Photographed under the supervision of Edward Steichen, 1944. The gradual fusion of raw recruits and a new ship into a formidable fighting unit. Shows the attack on Truk Island in the battle of the Philippine Sea.

The Fleet That Came to Stay, Department of the Navy, 1945. The story of the kamikaze attacks during the invasion of Okinawa and the role of the U.S. fleet in the invasion.

The Four Hundred Million, Contemporary Historians, Inc., Joris Ivens, dir. and script, 1938. The aggression of the Japanese Imperial Army against China.

Der Führer's Face, Walt Disney, 1943. Donald Duck is exposed to Nazi terror in this cartoon film.

Fury in the Pacific, Department of the Navy, 1945. The story of the landings on Pelelieu and Augur in the Palaus.

Fellow Americans, Office of Emergency Management. Garson Kanin, dir. James Stewart, narrator, 1942. The bombing of Pearl Harbor as if it had happened to four typical American cities.

Gas Racket, Office of Price Administration, 1943. Dramatization of the sale of counterfeit and stolen gasoline ration stamps to gasoline dealers.

The Grain That Built a Hemisphere, Walt Disney for the Coordinator of Inter-American Affairs, 1943. An animated story of the cultivation of corn in the Americas.

Hands, Signal Corps for the Department of the Treasury, 1944. A war bond promotion trailer.

Here is Germany, War Department, Frank Capra, prod., 1945. Made for the American occupation troops, the film reviews the history of Germany.

How Good is a Gun?, Signal Corps, 1944. An incentive film for munitions workers.

How Strong is the Enemy?, Office of Strategic Services, 1944. Estimates the industrial and military strengths of the Axis powers.

Inside Nazi Germany, March of Time, 1938. The first detailed news report on German politics shown in American movie theaters.

Is Your Trip Necessary?, War Activities Committee of the Motion Picture Industry, 1943. Asks citizens to restrict travel to make more transportation available for the military.

Japanese Behavior, Office of Strategic Services, 1945. Psychology and living habits of the Japanese people.

Japanese Relocation, Office of War Information, 1943. The forced relocation and internment of Japanese and Japanese-Americans in the U.S.

Just for Remembrance, Signal Corps for the Department of the Treasury, 1944. War bond promotion.

Justice, Department of the Treasury, 1944. War bond promotion.

Know Your Ally Britain, Army Signal Corps. Anthony Veiller, dir., 1943.

Know Your Enemy Japan, War Department. Direction begun by Joris Ivens and completed by Frank Capra, 1945. An analysis of the Japanese psyche and a capsule view of Japan's history, with an emphasis on totalitarian and aggressive behavior.

Last Stronghold, RKO-Pathé, 1940. A newsreel compilation which reviews events since 1914.

A Letter from Bataan. Paramount Pictures. William H. Pine, dir., c. 1943. Relates the nightblindness of a soldier in Bataan to the need to conserve food.

Let There Be Light, Signal Corps. John Huston, dir., 1946. The treatment and rehabilitation of servicemen psychologically disturbed by their war experiences; shows how they can return to the mainstream of American life.

The Liberation of Rome, Signal Corps with the cooperation of the British Services Film Unit, 1944. The U.S. and British campaign against the Germans from the landing in Sicily to the fall of Rome.

Lights Out in Europe, Herbert Kline, 1940. The Nazi attack on Poland; shows the capture of the Polish corridor and attacks on civilians.

The Memphis Belle, Army Air Force First Motion Picture Unit. William Wyler, dir., 1944. The story of a B-17 Flying Fortress on a mission over Wilhelmshaven, Germany.

Mission to Moscow, Warner Bros. Michael Curtiz, dir., 1943. Based on the book by Joseph E. Davies, U.S. Ambassador to the Soviet Union from 1936 to 1938; dramatizes the need for strengthening the U.S. alliance with the Soviet Union in the fight against German militarism and fascism.

Mr. and Mrs. America, Department of the Treasury, c. 1943. The price of war in men's lives; an appeal for financial support.

Mud and Soldiers, Marine Corps, 1943. A Japanese war feature film reedited to explain military strategy.

My Japan, Department of the Treasury, 1943. Designed to stimulate the purchase of war bonds; uses captured film to illustrate Japan's determination.

Nazi Concentration Camps, U.S. Counsel for the Prosecution of Axis Criminality, 1945. Documentary footage shot by Allied cameramen showing conditions in concentration camps at the time of liberation; used as evidence at the war crimes trials.

The Nazi Plan, U.S. Counsel for the Prosecution of Axis Criminality, 1945. A film history of the Nazi party, assembled for the war crimes trials.

The Negro Soldier, War Department, 1944. The black man's contribution to American life and culture and the participation of black soldiers in World War II.

The New Spirit, Walt Disney for the Department of the Treasury, 1942. An animated film about taxes and the war effort as explained by Donald Duck.

News Review No. 1, United Films/OWI, 1943. Worldwide wartime activities, December 1941—February 1943.

News Review No. 2, United Films/OWI. Helen Van Dongen, editor, 1943. Report on war events from all fronts.

Out of the Frying Pan Into the Firing Line, Walt Disney, 1943. A cartoon in which Minnie Mouse promotes the saving of fat scraps.

The Ramparts We Watch, March of Time. Louis de

Rochemont, dir., 1940. Through the experience of a small American town, the film reenacts the U.S. entry into World War I, drawing parallels to another approaching war. Concludes with German footage of the attack on Poland.

The Rear Gunner, Army Air Forces in cooperation with Warner Bros. Gordon Hollingshead, prod., Ray Enright, dir., 1943. Dramatization of the training and experience of a rear gunner.

Reason and Emotion, Walt Disney for the Coordinator of Inter-American Affairs, 1943. An animated film illustrating the duality of the human personality, with application to the conflict between democracy and fascism.

Remember These Faces, Department of the Treasury, 1945. War bond promotion.

Report from the Aleutians, Army Signal Corps. John Huston, dir., 1944. The U.S. Army Air Force campaign against the Japanese in the Aleutian chain; shows camp life among an isolated bomber squadron and concludes with the successful attack on Kiska.

Resisting Enemy Interrogation, Army Air Forces, 1944. A Hollywood-style training film illustrating how even the most innocent conversation between American airmen and their German captors can lead to disaster.

Le Retour (*The Return*), United Films (Franco-American production). Henri Cartier-Bresson and Richard Banks. The return of French prisoners from Nazi concentration camps.

Ring of Steel, Office of Emergency Management, Phil Martin, prod., Garson Kanin, dir., Spencer Tracy, commentary, 1942. A tribute to the American soldiers who have protected the United States since 1776.

Russians at War, Office of War Information. Helen Van Dongen, 1943. Behind the lines with the Soviets.

The Russian People, Helen Van Dongen and Joris Ivens, 1942. A compilation of Soviet war newsreels.

Safeguarding Military Information, War Department, 1941. Careless talk about military movements results in disaster.

A Salute to France, United Films. Jean Renoir, dir. Maxwell Anderson and others, 1945. Staged and documentary footage; French, British, and American soldiers discuss their experiences during war.

San Pietro, Signal Corps. John Huston, dir. and script, 1944. The cost in American lives to take an Italian mountain village from its German defenders.

Siege, Julien Bryan, 1939. The Nazi attack on Warsaw as filmed from the rooftops; shows the killing and destruction as well as the reaction of the refugees.

Silence, Signal Corps for the Department of the Treasury, 1944. War bond promotion.

The Stilwell Road, Signal Corps (Anglo-American production), 1945. The construction of a road linking Allied

forces in Burma and China. Retreat through the Burmese jungles and efforts to supply China by air and at the same time recapture Burma to set up bases.

Story of Big Ben, Pathé News for the Naval Bureau of Aeronautics, 1944. A tribute to shipyard workers.

Story of a Transport, Coast Guard, 1945. The transportation of the luxury liner *USS Manhattan* into a torpedo ship, the *Wakefield*.

Subject Germany, Signal Corps, 1945.

Target for Today, Signal Corps for the Army Air Force. William Keighley, dir., 1944. Explains the plans and purposes of the daylight precision bombing of Germany. Traces the development of the mission down to groups and squadrons.

This is the Philippines, Signal Corps, 1945. Philippine culture and geography, and the Japanese capture.

Thunderbolts, Army Air Force. Directed by William Wyler, 1945. The air war over Italy.

To the Shores of Iwo Jima, Warner Bros. for the Department of the Navy, 1945. Coordinated combat operations recorded on film to illustrate the cost of war.

Toscanini: Hymn of the Nations, Office of War Information. Irving Lerner, prod., Alexander Hamid, dir., 1945.

The Town, Office of War Information. Joseph Krumgold, prod., Joseph von Sternberg, dir., 1944. Shows the European traditions found in an average midwestern American town, with its eclectic architecture, mixed population, and many religions.

Troop Train, Office of War Information, 1943. The transportation of an armed division by rail as an object lesson to civilians who might complain about the difficulties of travel.

The True Glory, Signal Corps and the British Ministry of Information. Carol Reed and Garson Kanin, dir., 1945. D-Day, the Allied landing in France, and the victorious campaign in the West; features the men who fought the battles.

Two Down and One to Go, War Department. Frank Capra, dir., 1945. The army's point system of discharges to be followed after the defeat of Germany. Made for soldiers in Europe who believed they would soon be on their way home.

The War 1941–44, United Films. Worldwide war activities.

War Town, Office of War Information, 1943. The problems created by wartime industries for housing, education, medical care, etc. in Mobile, Alabama.

"Why We Fight" Series, War Department, 1943–44.

Prelude to War, Frank Capra, dir., 1942. The international events of the 1930s and the development of fascism, with a view to explaining the causes of World War II, particularly why the U.S. was fighting.

The Nazis Strike, Frank Capra and Anatole Litvak, dir., 1943. Shows the German advance toward the countries of Eastern Europe emphasizing propaganda, terror tactics, and strategy.

Divide and Conquer, Frank Capra and Anatole Litvak, dir., 1943. The German drive through western and northern Europe; the fall of Holland, Denmark, Norway, and France.

The Battle of Britain, Frank Capra, dir., 1943. Britain's resistance to and defeat of the German Luftwaffe.

The Battle of Russia, Anatole Litvak, dir., 1943. Russian history from the point of view that the Russians, who challenge the "invincibility" of the German forces, have always defeated and expelled the invading enmy.

The Battle of China, 1944. China's resistance to the Japanese invasion.

War Comes to America, Frank Capra, dir., 1944. The achievements and ideals of American society at stake in the war against fascism; shows the shift in public opinion from isolationism to support for entry into the war.

Why We're Here, War Department, 1944. An explanation of the Burma campaign.

With the Marines at Tarawa, Warner Bros. for the U.S. Marine Corps, 1944. Shows the heavy toll of American lives involved in the capture of Japanese-held Tarawa.

World at War, Office of the Coordinator of Government Films. Samuel Spewack, prod., 1943. Compilation of newsreels and captured footage showing world events, 1931–1942, with an underlying pattern of fascist aggression "inevitably leading to the attack on Pearl Harbor and the Western hemisphere."

The World in Flames, Paramount News, 1940. A documentation of events which set the stage for war. Argues the necessity for the U.S. to arm in defense of the democratic way of life.

Yalta Conference, Signal Corps, 1945.

You John Jones, MGM for the War Activities Committee of the Motion Picture Industry, 1942.

Notes on Color Plates
By Victor Margolin

CHAPTER ONE: GERMANY

(Page 41) Among the faces on this election poster are Hitler (modestly placed in the upper right-hand corner), Einstein (below Hitler), Mussolini (lower left), the world heavyweight champion Max Schmeling (next to Mussolini), and Hindenburg (center). Though Hitler lost the 1932 presidential election to Hindenburg, who won with 53 percent of the vote, he was asked to become chancellor of Germany in January 1933.

(Page 42) "Germans must choose between the bankruptors of the past and the men of the future." Goebbels is said to have had a hand in the design of this poster. Heinrich Hoffman, who did the photomontage, was Hitler's personal photographer.

(Page 44) Hitler was portrayed in this painting as a new messiah. The black raven of German mythology emanating rays of light is the satanic obverse of the white dove which symbolizes the Holy Ghost in medieval religious paintings.

(Page 45 Top, left) Einstein left Germany in 1933, the year he was forced to resign from the Prussian Academy of Sciences. Philip Lenard, a Nobel Prize physicist who had earlier scientific disagreements with Einstein, took advantage of his favorable position in the Nazi hierarchy to write in the *Völkischer Beobachter*, "The most important example of the dangerous influence of Jewish circles on the study of nature has been provided by Herr Einstein with his mathematically botched-up theories consisting of some ancient knowledge and a few arbitrary additions." The building off which the great scientist is being swept is the Einstein Tower in Berlin, designed by Eric Mendelsohn.

(Page 48 Top, right) The octopus was frequently used in wartime propaganda as an image of the aggressor. A French cartoon from the "Phony War" period shows Hitler as the octopus. Churchill as an octopus also appears in a German occupation poster for France.

(Page 52) Hitler's pose in this painted-over photographic portrait imitates a tradition of ruler portraits dating back to the Renaissance.

(Page 53 Top, right) This poster publicized a street collection for youth hostels organized by the *Verband Deutscher Jugendherbergen* (Association of German Youth Hostels).

(Page 53 Bottom, left) The "*Kraft durch Freude*" (Strength through Joy) organization was created to program the leisure time of German workers. Holidays, evening classes, and amateur cultural activities were planned, as well as massive sports and gymnastic events.

(Page 54) Hitler initiated a giant propaganda campaign to produce and sell a low-priced "People's Car." Over 300,000 Germans, under a gigantic layaway plan, started saving 5 marks a week (original cost: 990 marks, about $396). All told $67,000,000 was collected but the public never saw a single Volkswagen. The 300-odd prototypes found their way to the German General Staff. The first civilian Volkswagens were produced in 1945, after the war.

(Page 56 Top, right) Traveling exhibitions were considered an important means of propaganda by the Nazis. A major anti-Semitic exhibit was "*Der Ewige Jude*" (The Eternal Jew).

(Page 58) Though the SS under Himmler was originally formed as a security force, the Waffen-SS was introduced in 1940. Waffen-SS soldiers supplemented the Wehrmacht troops on both the Western and the Eastern fronts, and were guilty of some of the worst atrocities of the war.

(Page 60 Bottom, right) Posters such as this one, made from an academic painting of the Führer, were hung on the walls of offices and schoolrooms throughout Germany.

(Page 61 Bottom) One of a series of wall newspapers for use in offices and schools. Flechtner designed at least four other posters for the series, which probably began in 1938 and continued until at least 1943. Mjölnir and Hohlwein, among other artists, also did designs.

(Page 62 Top, left) The two lightning bolts form a V, the victory sign which the Germans co-opted from the Allies. The slain dragon as an image of defeated Bolshevism was also used on other posters. (See page 202, Bottom, right)

(Page 62 Top, right) *Feind hört mit* (The enemy is listening). was the German equivalent of Britain's "Careless Talk Costs Lives" and the United States' "Loose Lips Sink Ships." German "careless talk" posters always showed the hulking shadow of a spy in the background; the British took a lighter approach, using cartoons and puns. All the belligerent countries had posters to portray the "careless talk" theme.

(Page 62 Bottom, left) The legal category *Volksschädling* (enemy of the people) also comprised the *Feindhörer* (enemy listener) or *Schwarzhörer* (black listener)—people who listened to enemy broadcasts. After the German setback at Stalingrad, many people risked severe punishment by tuning in BBC broadcasts.

CHAPTER TWO: ITALY

(Page 90 Top, right) These stamps show Mussolini's preoccupation with Italian youth from birth to the time they were old enough to join the army.

(Page 93 Top, left) The Fascist fighter chips away single-handed at the Russian bear. Mussolini's braggadocio inflated Italy's role in combatting the Soviet Union. Italian volunteer legions, along with troops from France, Scandinavia, Belgium, Holland and other occupied countries helped bolster the beleaguered Waffen-SS troops on the Eastern front. (See Waffen-SS recruiting poster, page 93, Bottom, right.) But their presence was hardly influential.

(Page 93 Top, right) The wolf, symbolizing Italy, has fiercely ripped the British flag to shreds while suckling Romulus and Remus with kindness and love. This image of extremes suited the Italian temperament.

(Page 96) Like Mjölnir and other cartoonists, Boccasile used the black American soldier as an image of cultural barbarism, which he contrasted with the white marble Venus de Milo, an image of European classical purity on which a value of two dollars was placed.

(Page 99 Top, left) Goffredo Mameli (1827–1849) was an Italian patriot who fought with Garibaldi and died in the war of 1848–49. He was a poet and his song *"Fratelli d'Italia"* became a popular song of the independence movement. Mameli is used in this poster to establish a continuity between Garibaldi's "red shirts" and Mussolini's soldiers, to whose helmets are attached the wings of Hermes.

(Page 99 Top, right) Italian workers began going to Germany in 1940. At first they were attracted by the pay and working conditions, but they were treated as members of an inferior race. When they acted counter to Nazi discipline, they were severely punished; many were sent to concentration camps.

(Page 100) The Todt Organization was responsible for public-works projects in Germany. After Mussolini fell from power, the organization employed Italians on construction projects within Italy.

(Page 103) The "liberator" was also depicted as an agent of destruction in a German poster for occupied Holland (p. 201).

CHAPTER THREE: ENGLAND

(Page 125) Fougasse believed that humor would work better on beleagured Britons than stern exhortations. For Londoners on the run, he decided that simple images and phrases which could be absorbed at a glance would be most effective.

(Page 128) Posters by Games and other War Office designers were displayed in canteens, barrack rooms, medical huts, and other areas where soldiers congregated. Games, who was given a free hand with his designs, strove to elevate the graphic taste of the soldiers by his use of surrealist imagery, photomontage, and other techniques.

(Page 129) This poster was designed for the Ministry of Information's anti-VD campaign of 1943–44.

(Page 131) This poster symbolically depicted the Nazis as opponents of Christian values. The size of the cross in relation to the swastika affirmed that Christianity would triumph.

(Page 133) The hammer and sickle and the Star of David were used to imply Britain's domination by Bolsheviks and Jews.

(Page 136 Top) This curious piece of propaganda is drawn in the style of a Persian miniature. Roosevelt and Stalin, led by Churchill on a white steed, are chasing Hitler, Tojo, and Mussolini, who has been knocked off his horse by an arrow from Churchill's bow. The artist's calligraphic signature is next to the right foot of Roosevelt's horse.

(Page 136 Bottom) Sevek's streamlined style is reminiscent of Cassandre's posters of the 1920s and 1930s. The muscle-flexing giant signifies renewed British confidence after five years of hardship.

CHAPTER FOUR: UNITED STATES

(Page 165) This song was made famous by Spike Jones and his City Slickers.

(Page 170 Top) Shahn's poster refers to the forcible recruitment of French laborers to work in German factories.

(Page 173 Top, left) The face of Uncle Sam is that of the artist himself. The poster was published on September 6, 1944, three months after D-Day, and reflects the new confidence of the United States after a string of European victories.

(Page 173 Bottom) Rockwell's poster was issued soon after Bataan and Corregidor fell to the Japanese in the spring of 1942. It reflects the desperation of that period, when the United States was losing the war in the Pacific.

(Page 174 Top, right) Gaydos won second prize in the Museum of Modern Art's "United Hemisphere" Poster Competition in 1942. Each entry was to use one of twelve slogans expressing a new sense of unity in the hemisphere.

(Page 174 Bottom, right) Grohe's poster was used in factories but workers were uncertain whether the soldier was American or German, in spite of the German helmet. An Iron Cross on the helmet might have made the identity clearer but the poster's message, nevertheless, was not well defined. American designers had to learn that strong graphics were not necessarily as persuasive as more illustrative posters which hit closer to home.

CHAPTER FIVE: OCCUPIED EUROPE

(Page 193) The Rexist party was founded in Belgium by Léon Degrelle in 1935. René Magritte, the surrealist painter, reacted to the Fascist tone of Degrelle's propaganda by showing his image reflected in the mirror as Hitler. The poster was published by the Committee of Antifascist Intellectuals.

(Page 195 Top, right) The spirit of Pétain guides the collaborationist troops.

(Page 195 Bottom, left) The mother and child were common images on wartime posters. This poster shows them as victims of the ravages of war. A Greek War Relief poster (page 206 Bottom, left) showed them as symbols of courage and endurance. On a Canadian poster (page 169) they represented sacred values which the enemy would attack.

(Page 196 Top, right) The Germans used the specter of a Bolshevist onslaught to induce French workers to come to Germany.

(Page 199) The W. A. (*Wehrafdeling*, lit. defense division) was a paramilitary organization used by the Dutch occupation government as an auxiliary police force. The *Zwaarte Soldat* (*Black Soldier*) was the official W. A. publication.

(Page 202 Top, left) "Tout va très bien, Madame la Marquise" is the opening line of a popular French song. A servant first assures his mistress that all is well before proceeding to recount a long list of problems. The implication of this poster is that Churchill was offering the Europeans false hopes.

(Page 205 Top, left) The hand giving the V sign also looks like a dove of peace. The newspapers in the foreground—*Vrij!* (*Free*) and *La Libre Belgique* (*Free Belgium*)—were the leading resistance news sheets.

CHAPTER SIX: SOVIET UNION

(Page 225) This early anti-German poster shows the Russian worker struggling against a German aristocrat. The definition of the conflict in class terms, which reflects the influence of the Civil War, was later deemphasized. Russian wartime propaganda was based on loyalty to the nation rather than the party. The use of symbolism and the limited color range of red, black, and white typified Russian posters of the 1920s and early 1930s.

(Page 226 Bottom, right) The job of Russian propagandists in the winter of 1941 was to shore up the people's confidence that they would eventually repel the Germans. The huge hands and pincers of the Red Army express this confidence after the counter-offensive which shattered Hitler's plan to surround and capture Moscow.

(Page 227) The Russians, more than any other of Germany's adversaries, made Goebbels a prime target of their propaganda. Efimov drew him as Mickey Mouse with a swastika tail, Lebedev likened him to a braying donkey (page 238), and the Kukriniksi ridiculed him in numerous cartoons.

(Page 228 Bottom, right) As a parallel to the Soviet Army's winter counteroffensive in 1941–42 Ivanov and Burova's poster recalls the French defeat in the War of 1812. The figure in the background is Mikhail Kutuzov, the commander-in-chief of the Russian Army which compelled Napoleon and his troops to retreat from Moscow.

(Page 234 Top) To inspire the fighting forces, Russian propagandists recalled the exploits of the country's great military heroes. On the far left is Alexander Nevsky, who turned back the Teutonic Knights in 1242. Alexander Suvorov, in the center, helped defeat the Turks in the Russo-Turkish War of 1787–91, and Vasily Chapayev, on the right, led a Bolshevik division against Kolchak's anti-Bolshevik forces in the Civil War. He was killed in action in 1919.

(Page 235) The appeal to patriotic feelings for the motherland made Toidze's poster one of the most popular of the war. Stalin, in his "Holy Russia" speech of November 6, 1941, aroused his people's national pride by recalling the spirit of Russia's national heroes; generals like Donskoi, Suvorov, and Kutuzov, as well as eminent cultural figures such as Pushkin and Tolstoy. This appeal to the deepest feelings of the Russian people was more effective in bolstering their courage than any political rhetoric could have been.

(Page 239) When this cartoon appeared, the Russians had gained the offensive and could joke about Hitler's military strategy.

(Page 240) Ivanov's heroic figures typified the social realist style which dominated Soviet wartime posters. Although cartoons and caricatures were also used, the experimental graphics of the 1920s—the work of Rodchenko, Lissitzky, the Stenbergs, Prusakov, and Klutsis—had absolutely no influence on the visual style of the war years.

CHAPTER SEVEN: JAPAN

(Page 268 Top, left) Kimisaburo Yoshimura's *The Story of Tank Commander Nishizumi* (1940), which reflected the Japanese prewar humanist ideal, was one of Japan's greatest war films. It was excellent propaganda for the occupied countries because of its hero, a Japanese officer who was shown fraternizing with his men and aiding a Chinese woman and her child.

(Page 270 Top) The Japanese used a "divide and conquer" approach in their leaflet propaganda to Australian troops fighting on New Guinea and Papua. The Aussies were told that their women back home were succumbing to the advances of American and British soldiers while they were hacking their way through the New Guinea jungle.

(Page 273) The artist used the style of Milton Caniff, whose comic-strip characters "Terry and the Pirates" fought the Japanese throughout the war.

(Page 275) As a propaganda move to promote the Allied presence in China, Chiang Kai-shek was elevated to the status of The Big Three—Churchill, Roosevelt, and Stalin.

(Page 276) "Door gods" were small Chinese posters displaying figures from the Chinese pantheon. Rural families put them on their walls and changed them each lunar New Year. The China Division of the Office of War Information produced "door gods" for the Chinese peasantry which portrayed American aviators and preached Allied cooperation.

(Page 277) This poster appealed to the Dutch people to help break Japan's grip on the East Indies (See also page 279, Top, right).

(Page 279 Bottom, left) This leaflet, intended for Japanese troops and civilians, warned that the vast amount of Allied weaponry and manpower concentrated in Europe would be transferred to Asia. Japan's military leaders were blamed for the country's difficulties.

(Page 280) The original leaflet used the words "I Surrender" instead of "I Cease Resistance." It was unsuccessful because surrender was humiliating to the Japanese soldier. The wording on the second version avoided the stigma of surrender and had better results.

Bibliography

Altmann, John. "Movies' Role in Hitler's Conquest of German Youth." *Hollywood Quarterly*, v. 3, no. 4: 1949.

Anderson, Joseph and Donald Richie. *The Japanese Film: Art and Industry*. New York, Grove Press, 1960.

The Arts Inquiry. *The Factual Film*. London, Oxford University Press, 1947.

Auckland, R. G. *Aerial Propaganda Over Great Britain*. Sandridge, St. Albans, n.d.

Balcon, Michael, Ernest Lindgren and others. *Twenty Years of British Film, 1925–1945*. London, Falcoln Press, 1947.

Barnouw, Eric. *The Golden Web; 1933–1953 (A History of Broadcasting in the United States, v. 2)*. New York, Oxford University Press, 1966–1968.

Bartlett, F. C. *Political Propaganda*. Cambridge, Cambridge University Press, 1940.

Bellanger, Co. *La Presse Clandestine*. Paris, Armand Colin, 1961.

Blobner, Helmut and Herbert Holba. "Jackboot Cinema." *Films and Filming*, v. 3, Dec. 1962: 12–20.

Boelcke, Willi A., ed. *The Secret Conferences of Dr. Goebbels: The Nazi Propaganda War 1939–43*. New York, Dutton, 1970.

Bosmajian, Haig A. "The Role of the Political Poster in Hitler's Rise to Power." *Print*, May 1966: 28–31.

Bourget, Pierre and Charles Lacratelle. *Sur les Murs de Paris, 1940–1944*. Paris, Hachette, 1959.

Bramsted, Ernest K. *Goebbels and National Socialist Propaganda, 1925–1945*. Michigan State University Press, 1965.

Brenner, Hildegard. *Die Kunstpolitik des Nationalsocialismus*. Hamburg, Rowohlt, 1963.

Briggs, Asa. *The Birth of Broadcasting: The History of Broadcasting in the United Kingdom*. London, Oxford University Press, 1961–65 (v. 2).

Burden, Hamilton T. *The Nuremberg Party Rallies, 1923–39*. New York, Praeger, 1967.

Cannistraro, Philip. "*Il Cinema Italiano sotto il Fascismo.*" *Storia Contemporanea*, anno 3, no. 3, 1972.

——. "The Organization of Totalitarian Culture: Cultural Policy and the Mass Media in Fascist Italy." Ph.D. Dissertation, 1971. (University Microfilms)

Capra, Frank. *The Name above the Title: an Autobiography*. New York, Macmillan, 1971.

Carroll, Wallace. *Persuade or Perish*. Boston, Houghton Mifflin, 1948.

Causton, Bernard. "Art in Germany under the Nazis." *London Studio*, v. 12, Nov. 1936: 235–46.

Childs, Harwood, ed. *Propaganda and Dictatorship*. Princeton, N.J., Princeton University Press, 1936.

Childs, Harwood and John B. Whitton. *Propaganda by Short Wave*, New York, Arno Press, 1972.

Cole, J. A. *Lord Haw-Haw and William Joyce*. New York, Farrar, Straus & Giroux, 1964.

Courade, Francois and Pierre Cadars. *The Nazi Cinema: A History*. New York, Pitman, 1974.

Daskal, V. "Adventures in Art under Hitler." *Horizon*, v. 9, March 1944: 192–204.

Delmer, Sefton. *Black Boomerang*. New York, Viking Press, 1962.

de Mendelssohn, Peter. *Japan's Political Warfare*. New York, Arno Press, 1972.

Dickinson, Thorold and Catherine de la Roche. *Soviet Cinema*. London, Falcoln Press, 1948.

Dougherty, William E. and Morris Janowitz. *Psychological Warfare Casebook*. Published for the Johns Hopkins University and Johns Hopkins Press, 1958.

Dryer, Sherman. *Radio in Wartime*. New York, Greenberg, 1942.

Farago, Ladislas, ed. *German Psychological Warfare*. New York, Arno Press, 1972.

Fehl, Philipp. "A Stylistic Analysis of Some Propaganda Posters of World War II." M. A. Thesis (unpublished), Stanford University, 1948.

Field, John C. W. *Aerial Propaganda Leaflets*. Sutton Coldfield, England; Francis Field Ltd., n.d.

Fielding, Raymond. *The American Newsreel, 1911–1967*. Norman, Okla., Oklahoma University Press, 1972.

Fraser, Lindley. *Propaganda*. New York, Oxford University Press, 1957.

Furhammar, Leif and Folke Isaksson. *Politics and Film*. New York, Praeger, 1971.

Games, Abraham. *Over My Shoulder*. New York, Macmillan, 1960.

Gec, ed. *La Caricatura Internazionale durante la Seconda Guerra Mondiale*. Novara, Istituto Geografico de Agostini, 1971.

George, Alexander. *Propaganda Analysis: A Study of Inferences Made From Nazi Propaganda in World War II*. Evanston, Ill., Row, Peterson, 1959.

Goebbels, Joseph. *The Goebbels Diaries 1942–1943*. Edited and translated by Louis P. Lochner. Garden City, N.Y., Doubleday, 1948.

Grunberger, Richard. *The 12-Year Reich: A Social History of Nazi Germany 1933–45*. New York, Holt, Rinehart, & Winston, 1971.

Hadamovsky, Eugen. *Propaganda and National Power: The Organization of Public Opinion for National Politics*. New York, Arno Press, 1972.

Hale, Oron J. *The Captive Press in the Third Reich*. Princeton, N.J., Princeton University Press, 1964.

Hardy, Forsyth, ed. *Grierson on Documentary*. London, Faber & Faber, 1966.

Heiber, Helmut. *Goebbels: A Bibliography*. New York, Hawthorne, 1972.

Henslow, Miles. *The Miracle of Radio: The Story of Radio's Decisive Contribution to Victory*. London, Evans, 1946.

Higham, Charles and Jack Greenberg. *Hollywood in the Forties*. New York, Zwemmer/Barnes, 1968.

Hoffman, Hilmar and Peter Kress. "German Cinema of the Nazi Period." *Film Library Quarterly*, v. 5, no. 2, spring 1972.

Hitler, Adolf. *Mein Kampf*. New York, Stackpole, 1939.

Hovland, C. I., A. Lumsdaine, and F. D. Sheffield. *Experiments in Mass Communication*. New York, Wiley, 1965.

Howe, Ellic. *Studies in Psychological Warfare During World War II*. London, Rider & Co., 1972.

Hull, David. *Film in the Third Reich: A Study of the German Cinema 1933–1945*. Berkeley, University of California Press, 1969.

International Propaganda/Communications: Selections from *The Public Opinion Quarterly*. New York, Arno Press, 1972.

Jarratt, Vernon. *The Italian Cinema*. London, Falcon Press, 1951.

Kirby, Edward M. and Jack W. Harris. *Star-Spangled Radio*. Chicago, Ziff-Davis, 1948.

Knight, Arthur. *The Liveliest Art: A Panoramic History of the Movies*. New York, New American Library, 1957.

Konlechner, Peter and Peter Kubelka, eds. *Propaganda and Counter Propaganda in Films of 1933–45*.

Krabbe, Henning ed. *Voices from Britain: Broadcast History, 1939–1945*. London, Allen & Unwin, 1947.

Kracauer, Siegfried. *From Caligari to Hitler: A Psychological History of the German Film*. Princeton, N.J., Princeton University Press, 1947.

Kris, Ernst, Hans Speier, and others. *German Radio Propaganda: A Report on Home Broadcasts During the War*. London, Oxford University Press, 1944.

Lavine, Harold and James Wechsler. *War Propaganda and the United States*. New York, Arno Press, 1972.

Lean, Tangye. *Voices in the Darkness: The Story of the European Radio War*. London, Secker & Warburg, 1943.

Lee, Alfred McClung and Elizabeth Briant Lee. *The Fine Art of Propaganda: A Study of Father Coughlin's Speeches*. New York, Harcourt, Brace & Co., 1939.

Lehmann-Haupt, Hellmut. *Art under a Dictatorship*. New York, Oxford University Press, 1954.

Leprohon, Pierre. *The Italian Cinema*. New York, Praeger, 1972.

Lerner, Daniel, ed. *Propaganda in War and Crisis: Materials for American Policy*. New York, Stewart, 1951.

Lerner, Daniel. *Sykewar—Psychological Warfare Against Germany*. Cambridge, Mass., MIT Press, 1974.

Leyda, Jay. *Films Beget Films: A Study of the Compilation Film*. New York, Hill and Wang, 1971.

——. *Kino: A History of the Russian and Soviet Film*. New York: Macmillan, 1960.

Linebarger, Paul M. A. *Psychological Warfare*. New York, Arno Press, 1972.

Lockhart, Sir. R. H. Bruce. *Comes the Reckoning*. New York, Arno Press, 1972.

Low, David. *Autobiography*. New York, Simon and Schuster, 1957.

Malerba, Luigi and Carmine Siniscalo, eds. *Fifty Years of Italian Cinema*. Rome, Edizioni d'Arte, 1954.

Mandell, Richard. *The Nazi Olympics*. New York, Macmillan, 1971.

Manvell, Roger and Heinrich Frankel. *Dr. Goebbels*. New York, Pyramid Books, 1961.

——. *Films and the Second World War*. Cranbury, N.J., A. S. Barnes, 1974.

—— and Heinrich Frankel. *The German Cinema*. New York, Praeger, 1971.

Marcorelles, Louis. "The Nazi Cinema." *Sight and Sound*, v. 25, no. 4, autumn 1955.

Margolin, Leo. *Paper Bullets*. New York, Froben Press, 1946.

Meo, Lucy D. *Japan's Radio War on Australia, 1941–1945*. New York, Cambridge University Press, 1968.

Merton, Robert K. with Marjorie Fiske and Alberta Curtis. *Mass Persuasion: The Social Psychology of a War Bond Drive*. New York & London, Harper, 1946.

Millo, Stelio. "*Appunti sul Fumetto Fascista*." *Linus*, v. 2, no. 10, January 1966.

Moltmann, Günter. Goebbels' speech on total war, Feb. 18, 1943. In Holborn, Hajo, ed. *Republic to Reich: The Making of the Nazi Revolution*.

Mosse, George L. *Nazi Culture: Intellectual, Cultural and Social Life in the Third Reich*. New York, Grosset and Dunlap, 1966.

Nishimoto, Mitoji. *The Development of Educational Broadcasting in Japan*. Rutland, Vt., Charles E. Tuttle, 1969.

Padover, Saul K. *Experiment in Germany: The Story of an American Intelligence Officer*. New York, Duell, Sloan and Pearce, 1946.

Priestley, J. B. *All England Listened: The Wartime Broadcasts of J. B. Priestley*. New York, Chilmark, 1967.

Rolo, Charles. *Radio Goes to War*. New York, Putnam, 1942.

Rosengarten, F. *The Italian Anti-Fascist Press, 1919–1945*.

Rotha, Paul in collaboration with Sinclair Road and Richard Griffith. *Documentary Film*. London, Faber and Faber, 1952.

—— and Richard Griffith. *The Film Till Now: A Survey of*

World Cinema. New York, Humanities Press,

Rotter, V. "The War in Posters." *Art and Industry,* v. 39, Sept. 1945: 66–79.

Sadoul, Georges. *Le Cinéma pendant la Guerre, 1939–1945.* Paris, Denoel, 1954.

———. *French Film.* London, Falcon Press, 1953.

Sauberli, Harry. "Hollywood and World War II: A Survey of Themes of Hollywood Films about the War 1940–45." M. A. Dissertation, 1967.

Schockel, Erwin. *Das Politische Plakat: Eine Psychologische Betrachtung.* Munich, 1938.

Selz, Peter. "John Heartfield's Photomontages." *Massachusetts Review,* winter 1963: 306–336.

Seth, Ronald. *The Truth Benders.* London, L. Frewin, 1969.

Siepmann, Charles A. *Radio in Wartime.* New York, Oxford University Press, 1942.

Speer, Albert. *Inside the Third Reich: Memoirs.* New York, Macmillan, 1970.

Stedman, Raymond William. *The Serials: Suspense and Drama by Installment.* Norman, Okla., University of Oklahoma Press, 1971.

Stoetzer, Carlos. *Postage Stamps as Propaganda.* Washington, D.C., Public Affairs Press, 1953.

Tannenbaum, Edward R. *The Fascist Experience: Italian Society and Culture, 1922–1945.* New York, Basic Books, 1972.

Watt, Harry. *Don't Look at the Camera.* New York, St. Martin's Press, 1974.

White, John Baker. *The Big Lie.* London, Evans Bros., 1956.

Williams, L. N. and M. *Forged Stamps of Two World Wars.* London, 1954.

Wollenberg, H. H. *Fifty Years of German Film.* London, Falcon Press, 1948.

Wulf, Joseph. *Kunst und Kultur im Dritten Reich,* 4 v. Gütersloh, Sigbert Mohn Verlag, 1963–64.

Wykes, Alan. *Goebbels.* New York, Ballantine, 1973.

———. *The Nuremberg Rallies.* New York, Ballantine, 1970.

Zeman, Z. A. B. *Nazi Propaganda.* London, Oxford University Press, 1964.

Index

Credits

P. 11, (Bottom, left) Library of Congress. P. 17, (Bottom, left) Library of Congress; (Top, right) Library of Congress; (Bottom, right) National Archives; (Middle, right) Library of Congress. P. 18, (Top and bottom) Library of Congress. P. 19, (Top) Library of Congress. P. 21, (Top) Library of Congress; (Middle and bottom) Museum of Modern Art Stills Library. P. 25, (Bottom) Library of Congress. P. 26, (Top, middle and bottom) Library of Congress. P. 27. (Top) Harris Lewine Collection. P. 28, Library of Congress. P. 29, Library of Congress. P. 31, (Top and bottom) Museum of Modern Art Stills Library. P. 32, Library of Congress. P. 33, (Bottom) Library of Congress. P. 35, (Bottom) Library of Congress. P. 36, Musée Royal. P. 37, (Top and bottom) Herb Friedman Collection. Pp. 38, 39, Richard Merkin Collection. P. 40, (Top) Richard Merkin Collection; (Middle) Library of Congress; (Bottom) National Archives; (Bottom, right) Library of Congress. P. 41, Library of Congress. P. 42, Library of Congress. P. 43, U.S. Army Historical Collection. P. 44, U.S. Army Historical Collection. P. 45, (Top, left) Library of Congress; (Top, right) Library of Congress; (Bottom, left) Library of Congress; (Bottom, right) Imperial War Museum. P. 46, (Top, left) Library of Congress; (Top, right) Bundesarchiv; (Bottom) Library of Congress. P. 48, (Top, left) Library of Congress; (Top, right) Library of Congress. P. 49, Library of Congress. P. 50, (Top, right) Library of Congress. P. 52, Bundesarchiv. P. 53, (Top, left) Library of Congress. P. 55, Library of Congress. P. 56, (Top, left) Library of Congress. P. 57, (Top, right) Library of Congress; (Bottom) Library of Congress; (Top, left) Library of Congress. P. 58, Bundesarchiv. P. 59, Library of Congress. P. 60, (Top, left) Imperial War Museum; (Bottom, left) Library of Congress. P. 61, (Bottom) Imperial War Museum. P. 62, (Top, left) Musée Royal de l'Armée et d'Histoire Militaire; (Top, right) Bundesarchiv; (Bottom, left) Bundesarchiv. P. 64, Milton Cohen Collection. P. 67, National Archives. P. 71, Culver Pictures, Inc. P. 74, Culver Pictures, Inc. P. 75, (Top) National Archives; (Bottom) Museum of Modern Art Stills Library. Pp. 78, 79, (Entire spread) National Archives. P. 82, (Top) Milton Cohen Collection. P. 84, National Archives. P. 85, National Archives. P. 87, Library of Congress. P. 88, National Archives. P. 91, (Bottom, right) Milton Cohen Collection. P. 93, (Bottom, left) Library of Congress. P. 94, (Top, middle and bottom) Hoover Institution on War, Peace and Revolution. P. 95, Library of Congress. P. 98, (Top, left) Archivio Capitolino; (Top, right) Archivio Capitolino. P. 99, (Top, left) Archivio Capitolino; (Top, right) Archivio Capitolino. P. 100, Archivio Capitolino. P. 103, Archivio Capitolino. P. 104, Library of Congress. P. 107, (Top) National Archives. P. 112, (Top) Milton Cohen Collection; (Bottom) Herb Friedman Collection. P. 114, (Top) Imperial War Museum; (Bottom) Imperial War Museum. P. 115, (Top) Imperial War Museum; (Bottom) Imperial War Museum. P. 116, (Top and bottom) Imperial War Museum. P. 117, Museum of Modern Art Stills Library. P. 118, (All photos) Museum of Modern Art Stills Library. P. 120, Les Zeiger Collection. P. 121, Imperial War Museum. P. 122, (Top, left) Library of Congress; (Top, right) Library of Congress; (Bottom) Imperial War Museum. P. 123, Imperial War Museum. P. 124, (Top, left) Imperial War Museum; (Top, right) Imperial War Museum; (Bottom, left) Imperial War Museum. P. 125, (Top, left) Imperial War Museum; (Top, right) Imperial War Museum; (Bottom, left) Imperial War Museum; (Bottom, right) Imperial War Museum. P. 126, (Top, left) Imperial War Museum; (Top, right) Imperial War Museum. P. 127, (Top, left) Imperial War Museum; (Top, right) Imperial War Museum. P. 128, Imperial War Museum. P. 129, Imperial War Museum. P. 130, (Top, left) National Archives; (Bottom, left) National Archives; (Bottom, right) Imperial War Museum. P. 131, Imperial War Museum. P. 132, Library of Congress. P. 133, (Top and bottom) Milton Cohen Collection. P. 134, Library of Congress. P. 135, Richard Merkin Collection. P. 136, (Top) Library of Congress; (Bottom) Imperial War Museum. P. 139, (Top and middle) Library of Congress; (Bottom) Les Zeiger Collection. P. 140, (Top and bottom) Library of Congress. P. 141, (Top) Library of Congress; (Bottom) Culver Pictures, Inc. P. 142, (Middle) Library of Congress. P. 143, (Top and bottom) National Archives. P. 146, Herb Friedman Collection. P. 147, (Top and bottom) Les Zeiger Collection; (Middle)

National Archives. P. 148, (Top and bottom) Les Zeiger Collection. P. 149, (Entire page) Les Zeiger Collection. P. 154, (Entire page) Culver Pictures, Inc. P. 156, (Second row, right) New York Public Library. P. 158, (Top) Les Zeiger Collection; (Middle and bottom) Museum of Modern Art Stills Library. P. 159, (Top and bottom) Museum of Modern Art Stills Library. P. 160, (Top) Museum of Modern Art Stills Library. P. 161, Library of Congress. P. 162, Richard Merkin Collection. P. 163, San Francisco Archive of Comic Art. P. 164, (Top, left) National Archives; (Top, right) National Archives; (Bottom, left) Library of Congress; (Bottom, right) Library of Congress. P. 165, Les Zeiger Collection. P. 166, (Bottom, right) San Francisco Archive of Comic Art. P. 167, (Top, left) San Francisco Archive of Comic Art; (Top, right) Library of Congress; (Bottom) Copyright © Esquire Magazine. P. 169, National Archives. P. 171, National Archives. P. 172, (Bottom, left) National Archives. P. 173, (Top, left) National Archives; (Top, right) National Archives; (Bottom) National Archives. P. 174, (Top, right) National Archives; (Bottom, left) National Archives; (Bottom, right) National Archives. P. 175, (Top, left) National Archives; (Top, right) National Archives; (Bottom, left) National Archives; (Bottom, right) National Archives. P. 183, Musée Royal de l'Armée et d'Histoire Militaire. P. 185, (Top) Musée Royal de l'Armée et d'Histoire Militaire; (Bottom) Bibliotheque Nationale de Documentation. P. 186, (Second row, left) National Archives; (Third row, left) Musée Royal de l'Armée et d'Histoire Militaire; (Third row, left) Peter Robbs Collection. P. 187, Museum of Modern Art Stills Library. P. 188, (Bottom) Peter Robbs Collection. P. 190, (Bottom) Library of Congress. P. 191, (Top and bottom) Musée de l'Armée et d'Histoire Militaire. P. 192, (Bottom, left and right) Museum of Modern Art Stills Library. P. 195, (Top, right) Musée des Deux Guerres Mondiales; (Bottom, left and right) Musée des Deux Guerres Mondiales. P. 196, (Top, left and right) Musée des Deux Guerres Mondiales. P. 197, (Top, left) Musée des Deux Guerres Mondiales; (Top, right) Musée des Deux Guerres Mondiales. P. 202, (Top, left and right) Musée Royal de l'Armée et d'Histoire Militaire; (Bottom, right) Musée Royal de l'Armee et d'Histoire Militaire; (Bottom, left) Library of Congress. P. 203, Musée des Deux Guerres Mondiales. P. 204, (Top, left) Musée des Deux Guerres Mondiales; (Top, right) Library of Congress. P. 205, (Top, left) Musée Royal de l'Armée et d'Histoire Militaire; (Top, right) Musée Royal de l'Armée et d'Histoire Militaire. P. 206, (Top, left) National Archives; (Bottom, left) National Archives; (Bottom, right) National Archives. P. 208, Hoover Institution on War, Peace and Revolution. P. 217, (Top and bottom) Library of Congress. P. 219, Library of Congress. P. 220, Library of Congress. P. 221, National Archives. P. 223, National Archives. P. 224, Imperial War Museum. P. 225, Imperial War Museum. P. 226, (Top, left) Imperial War Museum; (Top, right) Library of Congress. P. 227, (Top) Imperial War Museum; (Bottom, left) Imperial War Museum; (Bottom, right) Imperial War Museum. P. 229, Imperial War Museum. P. 230, Imperial War Museum. P. 231, Imperial War Museum. P. 232, Library of Congress. P. 233, (Top) Library of Congress; (Bottom) Library of Congress. P. 234, (Top and bottom) Imperial War Museum. P. 235, Library of Congress. P. 238, Victoria and Albert Museum. P. 240, Imperial War Museum. P. 243, (Top) Library of Congress. P. 244, (Top, right) Imperial War Museum. P. 249, (Top) Library of Congress; (Bottom) Library of Congress. P. 250, (Top and bottom) Museum of Modern Art Stills Library; P. 251, (Top and bottom) Museum of Modern Art Stills Library. P. 262, (Top) Wide World Photos, Inc. P. 263, (Bottom) Wide World Photos, Inc. P. 264, (Bottom) Wide World Photos, Inc. P. 266, (Top, right) Library of Congress. P. 267, (Top, left) Hoover Institution on War, Revolution and Peace; (Top, right) Library of Congress. P. 268, (Top, left) Library of Congress; (Top, right) Library of Congress; (Bottom, left) Library of Congress. P. 269, Library of Congress. P. 270, (Top and bottom) Hoover Institution on War, Revolution and Peace. P. 271, Library of Congress. P. 274, National Archives. P. 275, National Archives. P. 276, Library of Congress. P. 278, (Top, left) Musée des Guerres Mondiales; (Top, right) Library of Congress. P. 279, (Top, left) Library of Congress; (Bottom) Library of Congress. P. 280, Library of Congress.

The text of this book was set in 12 point Bodoni Book,
named after Giambattista Bodoni (1740-1813).
Bodoni Book is a refined, delicate face
particularly appropriate for books and, as originally
set by the Linotype Company, is based on
a composite conception of the Bodoni manner.

PRODUCER AND ART DIRECTOR
Harris Lewine

DESIGNER
Seymour Chwast